Battlers & Billionaires

Battlers & Billionaires

THE UPDATED STORY OF INEQUALITY IN AUSTRALIA

Andrew Leigh

Published by Black Inc.
Wurundjeri Country
22–24 Northumberland Street
Collingwood VIC 3066, Australia
enquiries@blackincbooks.com
www.blackincbooks.com

First published in 2013; this updated edition published in 2024
Written on Ngunnawal Country

9781760645243 (paperback)
9781922231048 (ebook)

A catalogue record for this book is available from the National Library of Australia

Book design and typesetting by Marilyn de Castro
Author photograph by Hilary Wardhaugh

Printed in Australia by McPherson's Printing Group.

Contents

Introduction

One of the most brutal tests of national identity was described by Gavan Daws in his study of prisoners of war.[1] Looking at men who were 'barely functioning skeletons', beaten by their Japanese captors, weighing less than forty kilograms and surviving on less than a thousand calories a day, Daws imagined that national character would disappear.

Not so, he discovered. Among captured soldiers in World War II, Daws observed clear national patterns:

> The Americans were the great individualists of the camps, the capitalists, the cowboys, the gangsters. The British hung on to their class structure like bulldogs, for grim death. The Australians kept trying to construct little male-bonded welfare states. [Unlike Americans] Australians could not imagine doing men to death by charging interest on something as basic to life as rice. That was blood-sucking; it was murder. Within little tribes of Australian enlisted men, rice went back and forth all the time, but this was not trading in commodities futures, it was sharing, it was Australian tribalism.

Tom Uren, a prisoner of war who went on to serve in parliament, talked in his first speech about the difference between the Australian and British troops working on the Thai–Burma railway.[2] The Australians, under the command of 'Weary' Dunlop, mostly pooled their allowances from the Japanese (officers received more than other men). They lived 'by the principle of the fit looking after the sick, the young looking after the old, the rich looking after the poor'. By contrast, the British each kept their own allowance and divided up their tents according to rank. When the wet season came, cholera and dysentery killed all but twenty-five of the four hundred British men. As Uren put it, only a creek separated the camps, but it was the difference between equitable sharing and the law of the jungle.

Even the Australian military, one of our most hierarchical institutions, is infused with the nation's egalitarian spirit. Indeed, it has been suggested that this is one reason our forces are such effective peacekeepers. When the United Nations intervened in Somalia in the 1990s, Australian troops were more inclined to go on foot patrols than the French and US forces, who tended to stay in jeeps and behind sandbags. As a result, our troops were more likely to listen to local townspeople rather than just hearing the views of tribal leaders. This in turn made them more effective at solving local disputes. It was, as one account put it, 'an example of the traditional Australian sympathy for the underdog being put to very good use'.[3]

Egalitarianism goes deep in the Australian character.[4] Most of us don't like tipping. There aren't private areas on our beaches – getting a perfect spot on the golden sand depends on when you arrive. Audiences don't typically stand when the prime minister enters the room. When, as a federal member of parliament, I move around my electorate, my constituents will happily bail me up at the supermarket and swimming pool, the local café and running events. If a plumber drops around to fix the toilet, we'll offer them a cuppa. In Australia, it's quite normal to sit in the front seat of a taxi, but try the same thing in the United States and you'll soon find yourself dealing with a flustered cabbie.[5]

In January 1994, Los Angeles was hit by an earthquake and parts of Sydney were burned by bushfires. In the United States, the result was a tent city. In Australia, neighbours opened their homes to one another, with not a tent to be seen. Tim Flannery wrote, 'For the people of places like [the Sydney suburb] Jannali, the prospect of a tent city housing their neighbours would have been a deep insult to their sense of mateship. They would have done anything in order to avoid it.'[6] When Hurricane Katrina hit the United States, thousands were left stranded by the disaster. But not since the Great Depression has a crisis left large numbers of Australians living in shanty towns when other accommodation was available.

Our language has egalitarian cues. The word 'mate' is a universal leveller. I will say, 'Thanks, mate' to a cabinet minister and a bus driver – sometimes in the same day. The word 'sir' is now going out of fashion in the United States and the United Kingdom; but for at least two generations, Australians have used it only as a form of politeness, not deference.[7] In 2014, when the prime minister Tony Abbott reintroduced knights and dames, he was greeted with guffaws, and the decision was reversed the next year. Australians didn't want to start calling people 'sir' and 'madam'. The only knight I've ever known is one I thought of as a mate: my co-author on inequality Sir Tony Atkinson, whom you'll meet in the coming pages. The first governor of the Reserve Bank of Australia was called 'Nugget', and one of our billionaires is frequently referred to as 'Twiggy'.[8] If Jerome Powell and Elon Musk have similarly downmarket nicknames, they're keeping them extremely quiet.

Yet an egalitarian spirit is no guarantee of true equality. Indeed, as the nineteenth-century political philosopher Alexis de Tocqueville suggested, 'When inequality of conditions is the common law of society, the most marked inequalities do not strike the eye; when everything is nearly on the same level, the slightest are marked enough to hurt it.'[9] Tocqueville's point is that sometimes people in equal societies worry too much about inequality, while those in unequal societies worry too little about inequality. Put another way, just because we call each other 'mate' doesn't mean we have an equal distribution of incomes.

An important goal for policymakers is to ensure that economic gains are broadly shared across the community. Yet since the early 1980s, Australian inequality has increased significantly. That's true regardless of what measure we use. If we look at pay packets, the gap between the highest earners and the lowest earners has grown. If we look at total income (including investments in property and shares), inequality between the top income and bottom income groups has increased. And if we look at wealth, summing up the value of each household's assets – cars, homes, investments and the rest – then we see that the inequality gap between the richest and poorest has widened.

To see the full extent of inequality today, imagine that we conducted a parade of Australians, in which each person's height reflected their wealth. Suppose the parade lasted an hour, in which time all Australians walked past. In this parade, the average wealth would be represented by a person of average height. What would such a parade look like?[10]

The parade would begin with the subterranean people – those whose debts exceed their assets. They might tell an accountant that they are underwater, and they appear underground because they literally have negative net worth. Credit-card debt and payday loans are the reality for some living on the brink.

After a minute or so, people are above ground, but only barely. For about ten minutes, it is more like watching a parade of insects. Everyone is less than 10 centimetres tall. We are seeing people who have an old car and a few bucks in the bank, but no substantial superannuation savings and no property. Fifteen minutes in, and people are just 20 centimetres tall. They might work in fast food, childcare or as farm hands. They are more likely to live in outer-suburban or regional Australia.

At the half-hour mark, the people filing past are only 80 centimetres tall. The average household wealth in Australia is $1.5 million, but it takes until minute forty-three to see someone of average height. That's because wealth is massively skewed, with someone at the ninetieth percentile having sixty times more assets than someone at the tenth percentile. For most of the hour, the wealth parade resembles a parade of dwarves.

After we see average-height people, heights begin to soar. In reality, the tallest living person is a Turkish man who, at 2.5 metres, is too tall to play basketball. In the wealth parade, such giants appear at minute fifty-one. The rich cast shadows over the impoverished. In minute fifty-six, people in the parade are 4 metres tall, with household incomes of over $3 million.

Towards the end of the parade, things start to get wild. With one minute to go, people are 7 metres high. They have multiple investment properties and complicated share portfolios, and can afford to collect cars, art and jewellery. With half a minute to go, people are 10 metres high. Their household wealth is $9 million, almost the average house price in Australia's most expensive suburb, Bellevue Hill. We are entering the world of the super-rich, some of whom hold assets offshore, stashing cash in 'vulture funds' and 'opportunistic investment funds'.

In the final milliseconds of the parade, Australia's billionaires flash past. Their heads are literally in the clouds. The shortest billionaire is a kilometre high. The tenth-richest Australian is 16 kilometres tall – nearly twice as high as Mount Everest. At the very end comes Gina Rinehart, Australia's richest person. She is over 46 kilometres tall.

Jan Pen, a Dutch economist, invented the parade to remind us that the distribution of wealth is very different from the distribution of physical traits. We are quite similar to one another in size, looks and physical prowess, but our economic resources are vastly different.

'The rich are different from you and me,' said an awe-struck F. Scott Fitzgerald.[11] 'Yes,' replied the laconic Hemingway, 'they have more money.' Australia's first billionaires arrived in 1987, with Robert Holmes à Court and Kerry Packer vaulting past the billion-dollar mark.[12] In 2024, there were 150 billionaires in Australia.

Should we care? To see if you regard inequality as important, take this test. The pictures below show Australia's wealth divided into five pieces. Suppose that you had an equal chance of being in any of the five slices. Would you prefer Distribution I (where the richest fifth have 54 per cent of the wealth), or Distribution II (where they have 63 per cent)?

Figure 1: Which wealth distribution would you choose?

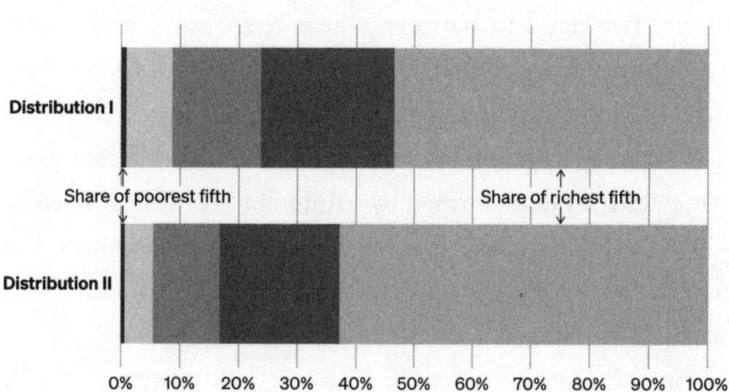

If you're like most people, you will opt for Distribution I. Not knowing where you might end up, you're behind what the Harvard philosopher John Rawls famously called the 'veil of ignorance'. This reminds me of the way my parents would divide up a piece of dessert between my brother Tim and me. If I got to cut, Tim got to choose. And here the result is the same: if you have to choose how to cut the pie without knowing which piece you'll get, you're likely to choose a fairer distribution. Oh, and in case you're curious, Distribution I shows how Australia's wealth was distributed in the mid-1960s. Distribution II shows how it is distributed today.[13]

Inequality isn't just to do with fairness – it also concerns how society can work most effectively. As rich and poor stretch further apart, the social fabric threatens to tear. This point was made most memorably by the British prime minister Benjamin Disraeli in his 1845 novel *Sybil*. Writing in a class-riven age, he described the affluent and the disadvantaged as being

> two nations; between whom there is no intercourse and no sympathy; who are as ignorant of each other's habits and thoughts, and feelings, as if they were dwellers in different zones, or inhabitants of different planets; who are formed by a different breeding; are fed by a different food, are ordered by different manners, and are not governed by the same laws.

The data bear out Disraeli's analysis. At the end of the nineteenth century, Britain was one of the most unequal nations in world history, with the top 1 per cent owning more than two-thirds of all wealth.[14] Today, that mantle has moved across the Atlantic Ocean to the United States. Life there has many admirable aspects, but rising inequality has begun to drive a wedge into the heart of US society. Wealthy Americans are increasingly opting to develop inefficient private workarounds for things that used to be publicly provided.[15]

When they're sick, some of the US super-rich turn to 'concierge medicine', which provides home visits and immediate access to specialists. Fearing crime, they may move to a gated estate, such as Florida's Indian Creek Island, accessible only via a well-guarded bridge to the mainland, and home to multiple billionaires.[16] If public libraries close, the rich can afford to buy their books and magazines. If there isn't an accessible public park, the rich can enjoy a nature walk by joining a private golf club. If local sporting facilities are inadequate, the richest can install a home gym or build a private swimming pool. And if the electricity grid goes down, the most affluent can switch to a backup generator.

In 2004, Democratic presidential hopeful John Edwards gave one of the best stump speeches of modern times, concerning the 'two Americas'. Like Disraeli, Edwards emphasised that splitting the country wasn't just bad for the poor; in the long run it would also hurt the rich.

In my work as a member of parliament, I'll occasionally meet people who find it hard to believe that any family could get by without a six-figure income, multiple cars, and children in private schools. From the outset, I know I'll have a tough time persuading them that they and their friends aren't typical. I don't begrudge them their affluence, but I worry at how little they empathise with how other people really live. Half of Australian households have an annual pre-tax income below $112,000. One in five households has an annual pre-tax income below $50,000.[17] In Double Bay (NSW), Toorak (Vic.) and Cottesloe (WA), average incomes are at least five times higher than in Elizabeth Park (SA), Broadmeadows (Vic.) and Myall Creek (NSW).[18]

Mining magnate Gina Rinehart, too, has sometimes seemed out of touch with her homeland. In a video message, she called on Australians to 'Do something to make more money yourself – spend less time drinking or smoking and socialising, and more time working'.[19] She has bemoaned the fact that Australia has to compete with Africa, where workers earn $2 a day, and called for a special economic zone around the Pilbara, with lower labour and environmental standards.[20] Doubtless Rinehart works hard, but few Australians have had a private plane at their disposal since childhood. And in the wake of Rio Tinto's destruction of the 46,000-year-old Juukan Gorge rock-shelters, few people are clamouring for lower environmental standards in the Pilbara.

One of the issues I'll discuss in this book is how the very rich make their money. Are they benefiting from hard work or a breakthrough innovation? Or are they earning what economists call 'rents': profits that are well above the cost of production, flowing from having monopoly power or some form of exclusivity?

Making this distinction isn't always easy, but one way to see it is to compare Gina Rinehart with her father, Lang Hancock.[21] At the time of his death in 1992, Hancock was worth $150 million.[22] In the 2024 rich list, Rinehart was worth $40.6 billion. Is Rinehart really 270 times more ingenious than her father? Not by her own account. She once said that 'Lang Hancock was the first person to observe and realise that in fact Australia could supply the total world consumption of iron ore'.[23] (Others have disputed the claim he was first, but I'll let it stand.) In explaining the vast wealth difference between Hancock and Rinehart, it's hard to ignore the substantial increase in the world iron ore price since 1992, delivering economic rents to Rinehart that her father could only have dreamed of.

For their part, the poor can often struggle just to get by. Poverty affects your life in myriad ways, from the very small to the very large. For example, if your household income exceeds $80,000, you're likely to be missing an average of three teeth due to tooth decay. But if your household income is below $20,000, you're likely to be missing ten teeth due to tooth decay. As a result, the poor have seven fewer teeth than the rich – an income gap that shows with every smile.[24] People in poverty are also twice as likely to have skipped meals or pawned something, and likelier to report being depressed, nervous or lonely.[25]

One of the most significant differences is in life expectancy. In a study conducted with the public health researcher Philip Clarke, I found that those in the richest fifth of the population could expect to live, on average, six years longer than those in the poorest fifth.[26] That's six more years that the rich have to travel, chat with friends, catch up on great movies and enjoy good food. Just by dint of being more affluent, the rich get six more birthdays with their grandchildren than the poor.[27] (In Chapter 5, I'll discuss the trickier question of whether other people's income also affects your health.)

In the table below, I've crunched data from recent surveys, splitting the sample into three groups based on household income, and comparing outcomes on a range of measures.[28] High-income adults are more than twice as likely to be employed and almost twice as likely to be partnered. The rich are more likely to be happy, have slightly better mental health and have much better physical health. By contrast, the poor are more likely to have experienced pain, to have been seriously ill or injured recently, or to have been a victim of violence. The poor are also more likely to have been to jail or have had a close family member jailed. This reflects the over-representation of poorer Australians among both victims and perpetrators of crime.

Table 1: Your money and your life

	LOW INCOME	MIDDLE INCOME	HIGH INCOME
WELLBEING			
Employed	37%	75%	86%
Partnered	45%	70%	75%
Satisfied with life as a whole	65%	68%	74%
Mental health score	69	70	73
Physical health score	71	84	89
PAIN AND VIOLENCE			
Experienced pain in the past month	83%	78%	75%
Seriously ill or injured in the past year	14%	9%	8%
Victim of violence in the past year	1.7%	1.4%	0.6%
Victim of property crime in the past year	3.2%	2.7%	2.5%
Self or family member jailed in the past year	1.7%	1.2%	0.8%
POLITICAL ENGAGEMENT			
Participated in a protest, march or demonstration	12%	16%	15%
Worked with others to express views	19%	26%	24%
Signed a petition	47%	55%	63%
Interested in the election campaign	72%	74%	81%
Political knowledge score	37%	39%	41%
GENDER AND RACE			
Female	53%	51%	49%
Aboriginal or Torres Strait Islander	5%	3%	2%

While it's true that some of the effects might run in the opposite direction (for example, being jailed makes you poorer), it's likely that most of what we're observing is the impact of poverty. That is what has been found in a series of studies looking at the impact of a sudden drop in income. Indeed, not having enough money can even affect your decision-making ability. Financial counsellors have long noted the damage that can be done when someone on the poverty line misses a credit-card payment, triggering punitive interest rates. An intriguing behavioural economics study suggests that poverty causes people to make decisions that aren't in their long-run economic interest.[29] When participants in the experiment were artificially given lower incomes, they were tempted to over-borrow at high interest rates. The end result was to increase the gap between rich and poor.

The poor are also more disengaged from politics. Low-income respondents are less likely to have participated in a protest march, worked with others to express political views, or signed a petition. Although government affects the lives of the poor more than the rich, it's the affluent who are most interested in election campaigns, and who tend to know more about how our political system works.

≠

This book is about economic inequality. In the main, I won't be talking explicitly about gender inequality, or the gaps between First Nations people and other Australians. But there's a significant overlap. In Table 1, I've shown the share of women and First Nations people in each of the three income groups. Women tend to live in poorer households than men. First Nations people are over-represented among the poor and under-represented among the rich.

Inequality also affects the gender pay gap. To see this, take a traditionally male occupation (banking) and a traditionally female occupation (teaching). If the pay gap between bankers and teachers widens, it will increase the gender pay gap – potentially offsetting factors such as falling rates of gender discrimination. If your main focus is the gap between men and women or the gap between Indigenous and non-Indigenous Australians, you should care about overall economic inequality too.

This is a book about inequality in *Australia*. In principle, we could look at inequality across cities or states. That would produce quite different results. For example, our most equal city is Darwin, and our most unequal is Sydney.[30] Some of the most equal places in Australia include Roxby Downs (SA), Palmerston (NT) and Ashburton (WA), while some of the most unequal include Gwydir (NSW), Cleve (SA) and Cottesloe (WA).[31] Over time, the geography of inequality has changed. A century ago, Australia's most unequal state was probably Victoria, with its goldmining wealth and company bosses.

Another approach would be to look at world inequality, comparing the incomes of the world's eight billion people. The distribution of incomes across the planet is much more unequal than the distribution in any one country.[32] The bottom half of the world's population receives just 9 per cent of global income and owns a mere 2 per cent of world wealth. Viewed from a global perspective, even poor Australians tend to be richer than the average African.[33] Global inequality is higher now than it was in the late nineteenth century, but it's fallen in recent decades thanks to rapid economic growth in China and India.

I've chosen not to focus on towns, states or the entire world because the first point of comparison for most of us is other Australians. This is partly a matter of empathy, as most people feel a strong affinity for their country. But thinking in terms of nations also reflects the practical changes that policies can make. Most of our taxes are raised at a national level, and the Australian government pays pensions and allowances to the neediest. Not all the levers that might affect inequality are at the national level (states have a good deal of influence over education, for example), but that's where most redistribution is done.

My discussion of the story of Australian inequality will start before the nation's founding. In the next three chapters, I discuss how inequality has fluctuated. Chapter 1 begins with First Nations Australians before English settlement and discusses the changes in inequality through to Federation. Chapter 2 picks up the story at Federation and discusses the 'great compression' that took place until the 1970s. Chapter 3 discusses the rise in inequality from the 1980s to the present day.

Once we know the contours of Australian inequality, we need to look at its causes and consequences. In Chapter 4, I look at how Australia matches up internationally and explore the main drivers of inequality. As an economist, I believe that big changes tend to be a function of events and policies, so the causes I'll focus on are technology, globalisation, taxation, unionisation and education. Chapter 5 analyses the consequences of inequality, looking at its benefits and costs – and busting a few myths along the way.

We cannot think about inequality without considering how things change over time. So in Chapter 6, I look at mobility and discuss the relationship between equality of opportunity and equality of outcomes. Chapter 7 then moves on to how Australians feel about inequality and redistribution. Are we happy with the existing gap between rich and poor, and do we want more social spending or lower taxes? Which values underpin inequality, and how does this play out in the political arena?

In our book, *Reconnected: A Community Builder's Handbook*, Nick Terrell and I find that community engagement has weakened over the past generation. Over recent decades, Australians have become less likely to join community groups, play organised sport or attend religious services. We have fewer friends and are less likely to know our neighbours. Australia has become less a country of 'we' and more a nation of 'me'.

As with community, so too with equality. As US political scientist Robert Putnam has noted, civil society tends to be stronger when income is distributed more equally. In the 1950s and 1960s, English-speaking countries were more community-minded and more egalitarian than they are today. But it would be foolish to think we should wind the clock back. So in the final chapter of this book, I look at a modern egalitarian agenda: how do we maintain an open economy but ensure that prosperity is widely shared across Australia?

1
First Nations to Federation

In 1770, Captain James Cook wrote of First Nations Australians that

> they live in a Tranquility which is not disturbed by the inequality of Condition. The Earth and Sea of their own accord furnishes them with all things necessary for Life. They covet not Magnificent Houses, Household stuff, etc; they live in a Warm and fine Climate; and enjoy every Wholesome Air.[1]

Was Cook right? In a sense, yes. When it came to economic resources, inequality among First Nations people was constrained by the necessities of subsistence.[2] One study of the eastern Gunwinggu people on the Gulf of Carpentaria estimated that getting 2000 calories a day (a bare minimum to survive) required everyone except the oldest, youngest and sickest to forage for nine hours a day in the wet season, and five and a half hours in the dry.[3]

Anthropological research indicates that some First Nations societies had rules on how food should be distributed; for example, a Worrorra man would give meat to his wife's parents, then to his own parents, and finally to everyone else.[4] When food was scarce, as it often was, the principle of generosity – backed up by ancestral law – often prevailed.[5] The simple reality was that even if a greedy hunter wanted to keep a whole kangaroo, it would quickly spoil. First Nations people developed a range of tools to obtain food (such as spears, digging sticks, harpoons and fish nets), but most groups were highly mobile and so did not need to invent techniques for large-scale food storage.

What was true of traditional First Nations Australian societies was true of hunter-gatherers generally. People in these societies had only as many possessions as they and their pack animals, canoes and sleds could carry. Typically, there was no such thing as private landownership. What was foraged from plants came in small quantities. Animal carcasses could not be kept for long. Hunter-gatherer societies in Africa, Asia, South America and the Pacific were extremely egalitarian, with less wealth inequality than any modern capitalist economy.[6] Imagine how much more economically equal Australia would be if each of us owned only what we could carry.

Yet small differences in resources between traditional First Nations Australians were offset by large differences in power.[7] It was an advantage to be male, older and a member of a more powerful social group.[8] Traditional First Nations societies often practised polygyny, with most permitting husbands to have up to four wives (the Yolngu people allowed twenty-six wives per husband, the highest recorded).[9] This led to considerable social inequality, even in a community with relatively little inequality of consumption or wealth. Food may have been pretty equally distributed, but sex was not.[10]

In the decades after colonisation, while living standards rose rapidly among British settlers, First Nations Australians saw few benefits and many costs. Their communities were devastated by diseases such as smallpox, tuberculosis, measles and the common cold.

Let's move now from the colonised to the colonisers, and take a look at the first colonial settlement, established in Sydney in 1788. The power imbalance between guards and convicts was colossal. As histories such as Robert Hughes' *The Fatal Shore* have taught us, the savagery of some of the early jailers was appalling. Yet the gap in material conditions among the settlers was modest. As Hughes put it, hunger was 'the hateful equalizer'.[11]

One study demonstrated this by analysing the extensive public records for Sydney from 1788 to 1790, which show the salaries of every soldier and civilian, as well as each person's food ration and clothing allowance.[12] After a price was put on the rations, inequality among the British settlers was estimated to be not only lower than has been observed at any other point in Australian history, but also lower than inequality in the United States, Britain and the Netherlands at that time.[13] Indeed, I had to look internationally to find a Western nation that at any point in its history was as materially equal: it was Sweden in the 1980s, at the high point of its egalitarian project.[14]

The early British settlers and First Nations Australians therefore shared a key trait: equality in resources sitting alongside massive differences in power. For both groups, income inequality was lower than at any time in the two and one-third centuries since colonisation. The reason for this was simple: both lived so close to starvation that sharing available resources equitably was the only way to keep people alive.[15] In a small society, it's hard to deny one person one meal a day so that someone else can have four. (Governor Phillip's early invitations to dine with him at Government House concluded with the request, 'Please bring your own bread.'[16])

Yet while Australia in the late 1700s had a fairly equal distribution of resources, this state of affairs didn't last long. The colony required entrepreneurs to provide goods and services, and many merchants came to hold monopoly positions and enjoy large profits from their frontier businesses.

Another factor was the distribution of land. While there was an initial attempt to distribute land equally, a few poor harvests quickly turned the focus onto maximising agricultural output. Because only a quarter of the convicts had farming experience, many enterprises faltered and governors increasingly gave more land to successful farmers.[17] Table 2 shows how the land share of the top 10 per cent and the top 1 per cent rose for selected colonial administrations between 1788 and 1821.[18]

Table 2: Rising inequality in colonial land grants

Governor / colonial administrator	Years	Share of land grants going to the top: 10 per cent	1 per cent
Arthur Phillip	1788–92	23.5	4.2
Francis Grose	1792–94	30.2	5.3
William Paterson	1794–95	25.1	6.8
John Hunter	1795–1800	44.2	10.9
Philip King	1800–06	59.3	15.3
Lachlan Macquarie	1810–21	57.2	12.8

From 1788 to 1821, the share of land going to the top 10 per cent more than doubled, and the share going to the top 1 per cent tripled. The most influential settlers received multiple land grants, including nine to William Balmain and seventeen to the Wentworth family (who received 5 per cent of all land granted under Governor Macquarie).[19] This suggests that political connections, not just productivity, shaped allocation decisions.

One way to see the growth of inequality in this era is to look at the rise of the super-rich. In his 2004 book *The All-Time Australian 200 Rich List*, William Rubinstein identifies the Australians throughout history whom he judges to have been the wealthiest.[20] The cut-off for inclusion is personal wealth of 0.17 per cent of national income, equivalent to $2.5 billion today. The list ranges from Samuel Terry ('the convict Rothschild') to present-day magnates such as the Westfield founder, Frank Lowy. From 1984 onwards, I add in anyone on the rich list whose wealth exceeds 0.17 per cent of national income.

In Figure 2, I have mapped the share of 'all-time rich-listers' who were in their last two decades of life in any given year since English settlement.[21] Because Rubinstein's list covers two centuries, you might expect to see the richest Australians spread evenly across this period, but the graph depicts a much more uneven pattern. The vast bulk of Rubinstein's all-time Australian rich list lived in the nineteenth century, with nearly a third in the 1820s. Note also the absence of anyone on the list from 1940 to 1980, and the return of the all-time rich-lister in recent decades. I will come back to this in the next two chapters.

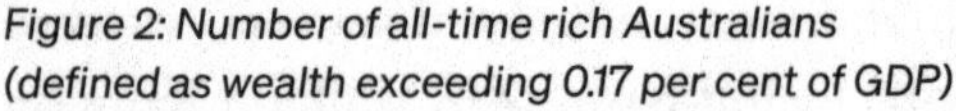

Figure 2: Number of all-time rich Australians (defined as wealth exceeding 0.17 per cent of GDP)

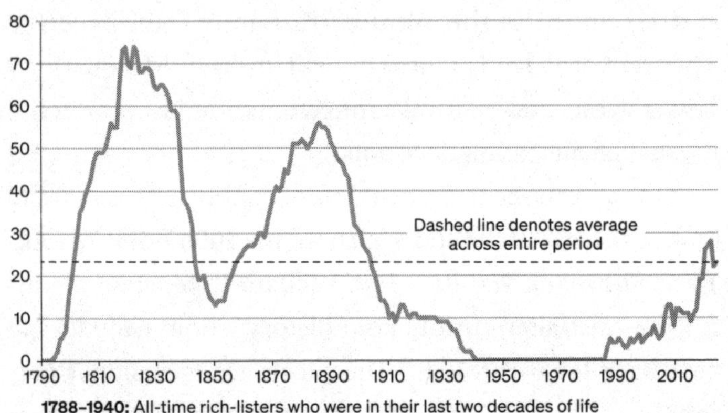

The key to nineteenth-century inequality was property. As Charles Darwin noted when he visited Australia in 1836: 'The whole population, poor and rich, are bent on acquiring wealth: amongst the highest orders, wool and sheep-grazing form the constant subject of conversation.'[22] In 1844, the top 0.1 per cent owned a whopping 17 per cent of land, and 11 per cent of all livestock.[23]

Yet as Figure 2 shows, inequality in nineteenth-century Australia fluctuated. The graph of all-time rich-listers peaks in 1820, but then falls mid-century. This pattern shows up in other data too. Although we do not have regular income surveys and taxation statistics for this period, we can assess inequality by asking: how many days' work were required to buy a hectare of land? As economic historian Jeffrey Williamson explains, 'in a world where the agricultural sector was big and where land was a critical component of total wealth', this is revealing: 'It tells us how the typical landlord at the top of the distribution did relative to the typical unskilled (landless) worker near the bottom.'[24]

The measure captures the economic resources of employees versus landlords. When fewer days of work were required to buy a hectare of land, workers could hope to make the jump into the landed class. When the requisite number of work days was greater, property ownership was out of the question, and paying the rent took up a larger share of a worker's pay packet. In Chapter 3, we will look at a similar measure: the number of years of work needed to buy a house.

To put the historical data in context, let's look at the number of days' work required to buy a hectare of land today. (Note that with this metric we are referring to land, not homes, and most land is not in cities. A hectare of land in remote Australia is much cheaper than a house in the suburbs.) Dividing average weekly wages by seven, average daily earnings for full-time adults come out at around $270, while a hectare of farmland costs around $4700.[25] So an average full-time worker today would need to work for seventeen days to buy a hectare of farmland (ignoring taxes).

Turning back to the past, the period from 1820 to 1870 was characterised by rapid growth in per-person incomes, which grew twice as fast as in the United States and three times faster than in the United Kingdom.[26] Moreover, Jeffrey Williamson and economic historian Laura Panza argue that this period witnessed an egalitarian revolution. Freed convicts became wage-earners and moved up the earnings ladder. Large-scale land settlement made property less scarce, and lowered its relative value.

In Figure 3, the first line – running from the 1820s to the 1870s – uses data from Panza and Williamson. It shows how long an unskilled worker had to toil to buy a hectare of land. This number peaks in 1835 at fifty-four days before dropping to just nine days in 1871. This implies that an unskilled worker in 1871 could buy six times as much land with their pay packet as they could have done thirty-six years earlier. Australia's national bard, Les Murray, once described European settlers to Australia as 'the poor who got away'.[27] And it was indeed a great escape – while in land-scarce Europe most labourers could never dream of affording a plot of land, by the 1870s it was within reach for the typical Australian worker.

Figure 3: Number of days work required to buy a hectare of land

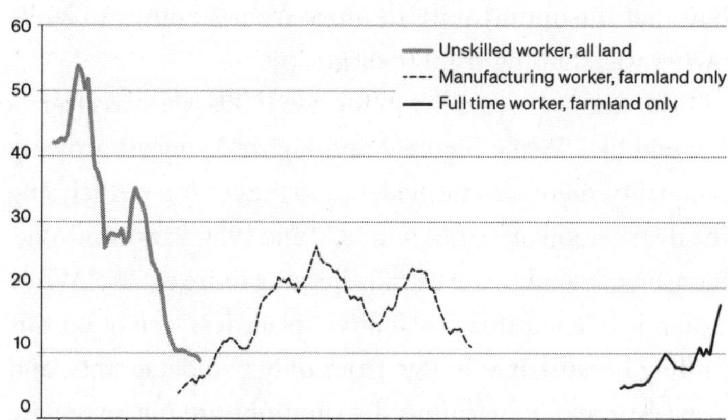

Based on slightly different data sources, the second line, running from the 1860s, shows the number of days a manufacturing worker had to toil to buy a hectare of farmland. Compared with the first series, this metric looks at better-paid workers and cheaper land. Accordingly, when the first two lines overlap in the 1860s, the second line is slightly below the first one. It starts in 1865, when the average daily wage of a manufacturing worker was £0.18 and a hectare of farmland cost £0.74, or four days' toil.[28] Over the ensuing decades, the cost of land rapidly outpaced average earnings with wages hit hard in the 1890s depression.[29] By 1901, the average daily wage had only increased to £0.19, while a hectare of farmland cost £3.90, or twenty days' work. By 1905, it took twenty-six days' wages to buy a hectare of farmland. This measure of inequality suggests that Australia became more unequal during the final decades of the nineteenth century. It implies that many workers would have felt the opportunity to move from labourer to landowner was slipping from their grasp.

The story of inequality in the late 1800s is not as clear as I would like. While Figure 2 and Figure 3 suggest growing inequality, there is some evidence to the contrary. Analysing the distribution of earnings in 1870 and 1910, Panza and Williamson contend that Australia became more equal.[30] While I do not rule out this possibility, I place less weight on this finding because it is drawn from only two datapoints, and their estimates of earnings distributions are not as precise as one might hope. On balance, my assessment is that Australian inequality rose in the late 1800s, but I remain open to revisiting this view if further evidence comes to light.

Just as it does today, a vast divide existed between toilers and tycoons in the late nineteenth century. To get a sense of the gap – and the role of property ownership – let's look at the stories of two nineteenth-century Australians, Richard Casey and Jock Neilson.

Born in 1846, the son of a Tasmanian doctor, Richard Casey became a jackeroo at age seventeen and quickly rose to managing sheep stations in the Riverina. Casey experienced a setback when he and his business partners were unable to repay their creditors in the depression of the 1890s. However, he was quickly off to the Western Australian goldfields, where he managed to profit handsomely from the sale of shares in a mine that turned out to contain little gold.

Back in Melbourne, Richard Casey became a company director and investor. He built a thirty-five-room home on a hectare of land in South Yarra, bought his cigars five hundred at a time and engaged an entourage of servants. He bought racehorses, chaired the Victorian Racing Club and wore suits made in London. Casey was a member of the most exclusive clubs in Sydney, Melbourne and Brisbane, married the daughter of a Brisbane merchant and associated with rich businessmen like himself.

A little younger than Casey, Jock Neilson was the first of eight children. Alongside his father and brothers, he worked as a bush labourer: timber-cutting, making roads or fixing fences. His sisters worked as servants for rich farmers. The Neilson family built their own home, which had an earth floor and was lined with hessian. Meals were cooked on a camp oven and the room lit by 'slush lamps' that burned animal fat. In 1895, the family tried to fence their land to keep the rabbits out, but by the time they got it done the crop had been eaten. Neilson's mother died of typhoid, and he lost a brother and a sister to tuberculosis.

Visiting Australia in the late nineteenth century, the English novelist Anthony Trollope was struck by the fact that 'the bulk of the labour is performed by a nomad tribe, who wander in quest of their work, and are hired only for a time'.[31] This description fitted Jock Neilson perfectly. His life consisted of tramping through western Victoria, looking for odd farm jobs. He sheared sheep, picked grapes, made fences and – perhaps toughest of all – dug mallee roots out of fields ('mallee grubbing'). He estimated that, over a thirty-year period, he had more than two hundred employers.

Late in life, Jock Neilson finally found an audience for the lyric poems he liked to compose while working. His poems often dealt with the themes of hard work and poverty:

> The weather's hot and horrid
>   and the old man's got the blight,
> The grain is small and shrivelled
>   and the bags are very light,
> The rain may come tomorrow
>   and knock the whole lot down
> And last night came a letter
>   from the mortgagees in town.

The stories of Richard Casey and Jock Neilson are told by historian Stuart Macintyre, who notes the 'colossal' extremes of wealth and poverty of the era, and points out that Casey would have been several thousand times wealthier than Neilson.[32] The differences manifested themselves in their housing, health and even mode of travel: while Neilson walked up to a thousand miles in a journey, Casey travelled first class by ship to London whenever he wished.

Wealth provides an insurance policy in the face of a crisis. In the classic Australian novel *Power Without Glory*, Frank Hardy writes of the late-nineteenth-century downturn:

> Unemployment grew to alarming proportions. Bewilderment and panic gripped the speculators, business men and bankers; starvation and despair gripped the workless. The Trade Unions resisted with a series of

> strikes, culminating in the maritime strike of 1890 … John West [the central character in the novel] was sacked, together with most of the other boot workers. The West family sank with their kind deeper into the mire of poverty.[33]

Note the different impact here. While bankers suffered panic, boot workers suffered poverty.

Another useful measure of social equity is the share of people working as domestic servants. The historian Barry Higman observed that when income gaps are large, societies will have more domestic servants.[34] There is always demand for such servants – the question is whether people can afford to hire them.

On this measure, inequality was extremely high in the nineteenth century, with nearly 4 per cent of Australians working as domestic servants in 1861 (to put this into perspective, this is a larger share of people than currently work as schoolteachers). Half of all employed women were servants. The fraction of Australians working as servants fell to 3 per cent in 1901, and 2 per cent in 1921. Nonetheless, these numbers still reflect a high level of domestic servitude. Servants would compose only 1 per cent of the population in 1947, and would then drop to almost zero over the next few decades.[35] (As I will note below, servants are now making a comeback, albeit in a different form.)

If we were to take a time machine back to nineteenth-century Australia, the extremes of wealth would remind us more of Dickens' London than the nation of today. Land was expensive, servants were abundant, and the divide between rich and poor was vast. The historian John Hirst points out that policemen were instructed to salute gentlemen dressed in frockcoats and top hats, and letters to such men were always addressed 'Esquire'.[36]

Penned on the eve of the twentieth century, Henry Lawson's poem 'For'ard' describes the class distinctions on a steamship.[37] The 'for'ard' section houses the 'second-classers', who are 'stowed away like sheep'. In the aft section, the gentry travel in 'cushioned cabins' with 'saloons 'n' smoke-rooms'. Women in the for'ard section are fed separately, 'Just as if they couldn't trust 'em for to eat along with us!', while the gentlemen and ladies 'always dine together, aft'. Separating the two groups, a sign in the middle of the ship 'says that second-classers ain't allowed abaft o' this'.

Lawson yearns for a time when 'the curse o' class distinctions from our shoulders shall be hurled ... When the people work together, and there ain't no fore-'n'-aft.' How much would these ideals be realised in the twentieth century, when a new nation was born?

2
Federation to the 1970s – the Great Compression

After the recessions and droughts of the 1890s, Federation in 1901 brought with it a sense of excitement and possibility. W.K. Hancock sums up the spirit of the era as imbued with 'the sentiment of justice, the claim of right, the conception of equality'.[1] Yet the rhetoric of equality had clear limits. In September 1901, Prime Minister Edmund Barton told the federal parliament: 'I do not think that the doctrine of the equality of man was really ever intended to include racial equality.'[2] This attitude echoed that of the US founding fathers, who wrote in the Declaration of Independence that 'all men are created equal', but kept their slaves. Support for equality in Australia was stronger in word than deed, and division according to gender and race remained entrenched and official.

Just as in the nineteenth century, there was a good deal of economic inequality. Large fortunes were made in the early decades of the twentieth century, and many of the super-rich lived extravagantly.[3] The retail merchant Samuel

Hordern lived the high life in Sydney, racing yachts and breeding racehorses. The goldmining millionaire Walter Hall was also a racehorse owner, and his Potts Point mansion was filled with old master paintings. Samuel McCaughey had a 1.3-million-hectare pastoral empire in the Riverina, and angered downstream farmers by damming rivers that flowed through his property.

Yawning social gaps meant that great deference was paid to the elite. They coveted membership of the exclusive Melbourne Club or the Australian Club in Sydney: both founded in 1838, and both of which exclude women members to this day. In New South Wales and Queensland, the state upper houses were appointed, not elected – and only 'gentlemen' were seriously considered in most cases. This was a world apart from how the poorest Australians lived.

Two early clashes between the classes occurred in 1907. The first saw the millionaire farm-machine manufacturer Hugh McKay compelled to pay 'fair and reasonable' wages. In a case that came to be known as the Harvester judgment, the Commonwealth Conciliation and Arbitration Court ruled that employees were entitled to seven shillings a day, a wage that would keep an average family out of poverty.[4] The case was celebrated by the union movement, and by the Australian Labor Party, which had been formed in 1891.

1907 also saw the formation of the NSW Rugby Football League, which broke away from Rugby Union over the issue of player payments.[5] Traditionally, Union had enforced amateurism. That was fine for affluent players, but working-class men could not take time off to train and play without receiving compensation. Again, the working classes had a win, with professionalised Rugby League soon displacing Union in New South Wales and Queensland. Current and future Labor politicians were among League's early leaders.[6] H.V Evatt, who would go on to lead the Labor Party nationally, served as one of the founders of Sydney University's Rugby League club. When he first ran for the electorate of Balmain, Evatt advertised in the official Rugby League journal that he was 'the Rugby League candidate'.

≠

And yet the gap between rich and poor remained large. The minimum (or 'basic') wage was around £100 a year, less than US labourers of the era were earning, but a little more than their counterparts in the United Kingdom.[7] With even a bungalow in a cheap suburb costing £800, home ownership was out of reach for many.[8] The housing stock was also of much lower quality than today: in the 1910s, more than half of Australia's houses had wooden walls.[9]

Life for many Australians was hard in the Downton Abbey era. At the outbreak of World War I, it still took nineteen days' wages for a manufacturing worker to buy a hectare of farmland. At this time, many Australians would have been conscious of living in a country where the rich were doing considerably better than the rest.

Australia at this time was more egalitarian than Britain, but the class divides were substantial nonetheless. When

400,000 men enlisted to fight in World War I, many owned nothing beyond what they carried. The First Australian Imperial Force included considerable numbers of men who had been unemployed.[10]

On the home front, the outbreak of World War I was particularly felt by the poorest. The closure of European markets and the cessation of British loans caused mass lay-offs in export industries, such as timber and coalmining, and caused many public-works programs to stop. Through 1914, unemployment rose from 6 to 11 per cent. The hardship continued the following year. Because wages were restricted but prices were not, the real wage fell by 10 per cent from 1914 to 1915.[11] The ferocity of class conflict in the era can be seen in the number of working days lost to strikes: five million in 1917 alone, or two and a half days for every worker.[12]

Despite their sacrifice, many returning soldiers faced bleak employment prospects. Into the 1920s, most men commuted by foot or bicycle, children wore hand-me-downs, people washed once a week in a tub, and doctors were only for emergencies. Stuart Macintyre quotes one account of the staple diet of such families:[13]

> white bread with either dripping, jam or treacle, and tea. There is a certain amount of meat scraps and potatoes, perhaps rice occasionally, but the staple diet the children get, two or three times a day, is such as I have described.

In the last chapter we had to rely on fairly crude eighteenth- and nineteenth-century measures of inequality, such as the number of magnates, the number of people working as servants, and the relationship between wages and land prices. But as we come closer to the present day, the quality and range of inequality measures steadily improves. Indeed, Australian data for the early twentieth century are surprisingly good for the era. Corrado Gini, the Italian statistician who was one of the founders of the study of inequality, drew on earnings, incomes, inheritances and land values collected in the 1910s by the state of Victoria in devising the measure known as the 'Gini coefficient'.[14] A Gini of zero means a perfectly equal society, while a Gini of one means a perfectly unequal society, in which a single person has all the resources.

One way that we can learn about inequality in the twentieth century is by considering the share of income received each year by the top earners. Although direct surveys of income were relatively rare, income taxes had been introduced in several states by the early twentieth century, and authorities regularly published tabulations of tax returns.

The idea of using taxation statistics to analyse inequality has a long lineage, but only relatively recently has it been properly refined.[15] In crunching the figures, I teamed up with an Oxford University economist, Sir Tony Atkinson, and together we dug through dusty yearbooks and annual reports to compile a picture of inequality from the early twentieth century onwards. More recently, these data have been compiled by economist Roger Wilkins. This methodology allows us to answer questions such as 'What was the income share of the top 1 per cent of Australian adults?' Figure 4 shows the answer to this question, spanning the period from 1912 to 2020, the most recent year for which taxation statistics are available (for simplicity, tax years are represented by their starting year, so 1942–43 is simply 1942).

Figure 4: Top income shares

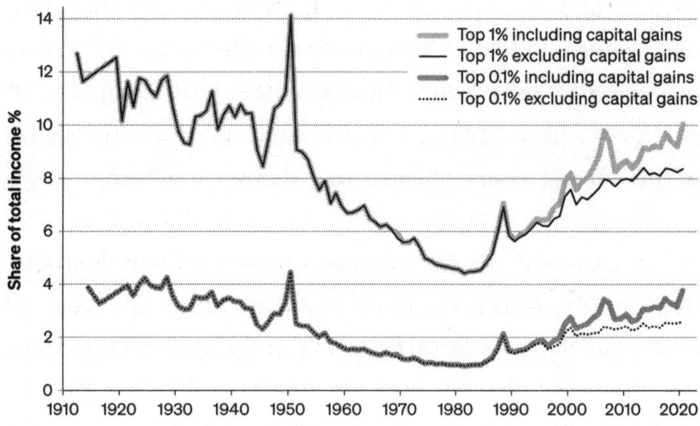

Let's start with the top 1 per cent, 'the affluent', who would be defined in 2020 as people with pre-tax incomes over about $275,000. In the 1910s, the affluent received 12 per cent of all personal income – twelve times their proportionate share. With the exception of a brief spike caused by the Korean War wool boom, the top 1 per cent's share in the era of World War I was higher than at any other point of the twentieth century.[16]

The pattern is similar for the top 0.1 per cent, 'the opulent'. In 2020, you needed an annual pre-tax income exceeding $935,000 to be in the top one-thousandth of income earners. As the lower line in Figure 4 shows, the opulent in the 1910s and 1920s had around 4 per cent of all household income – or forty times their proportionate share.

The time of greatest economic hardship was the Great Depression of the 1930s. In the first year of the Depression, Australia's national income fell by 8 per cent.[17] In 1931, the Arbitration Court reduced all award wages by 10 per cent and the federal government cut the aged pension by 12.5 per cent.[18] There was talk of 'equality of sacrifice', but top income shares did not fall much. Those who suffered most were the one-third of men who were unable to find work in 1932, the families that struggled to stay together, the hundreds of people who slept in the Sydney Domain, and the children who went to school malnourished.[19] While some of the super-rich gave generously, many charities struggled to raise resources. Average real earnings in the late 1930s were no higher than they had been in the late 1920s.[20]

World War II marked an important shift in the social compact, partly because so many citizens had vivid memories of living through World War I. In 1939, unlike in 1914, there was widespread recognition of the massive sacrifice that war entailed, and a strong belief that the burden must be shared fairly across the community. Prime Minister John Curtin told parliament in 1942: 'there will have to be a fairer distribution of wealth'.[21]

Various measures were put in place to achieve this. Prices and rents were controlled so that workers did not see their costs escalating while their wages were frozen. Ration cards were introduced for basic foodstuffs and clothing.[22] Income taxes were federalised and the tax base expanded so that the typical worker paid federal income tax for the first time. Tax rates were increased for high earners as well, with the top marginal tax rate reaching 93 per cent in the latter years of the war. The effect of all these changes was to reduce the after-tax incomes of the rich and boost the buying power of the poor.

As the government's 1945 white paper on full employment noted:

> On the average during the twenty years between 1919 and 1939 more than one-tenth of the men and women desiring work were unemployed ... [W]ar-time full employment ... has shown up the wastes of unemployment in pre-war years, and it has taught us valuable lessons which we can apply to the problems of peacetime, when full employment must be achieved.[23]

In 1947, the Australian Council of Trade Unions successfully persuaded the Arbitration Court to rule for a forty-hour working week. The government directly created jobs, quadrupling the size of the federal public service between 1939 and 1951.[24] Home ownership rates rose significantly, with 200,000 homes built between 1945 and 1949.[25] The price of cars continued to fall relative to wages, and the number of cars increased by 450,000. On one estimate, an employee at the end of the 1940s would have needed to work for two years on the minimum wage to afford a new Holden sedan.[26] By the mid-1960s, the price of a new Holden was down to a year's minimum wage.

Census and survey figures are not as plentiful for the past as for today, but at certain moments of crisis (1915, 1933 and 1943), the Australian Bureau of Statistics decided to ask about incomes.[27] In 1969, the ABS carried out a sample survey of incomes. Putting this handful of observations together shows clearly that inequality fell from the 1930s to the 1960s.[28] Gaps across occupations narrowed too. One study of NSW wages found that at the time of Federation, unskilled workers earned £0.71 for every pound a skilled worker took home.[29] By 1938, this had ticked up to £0.80. By 1957, it was £0.91.

The Australian education system also saw improvements in the post-war decades. These were partly spurred by the recognition that in some cases our schools had failed to produce military recruits who could read and write. One in twenty of the Australian soldiers who fought in World War II was functionally illiterate, and many more had low literacy levels.[30]

For some, having served in the war meant a scholarship to attend university. One of these men was my paternal grandfather, Keith Leigh, who could not have paid the fees for the University of Melbourne on his modest clergyman's wage. For thousands of men like Keith, the end of the war brought new opportunities. Post-war Australia did not have enough high-school graduates to create a university revolution on the scale of the US 'GI Bill', but it nonetheless expanded access to many more young men.

Post-war Australia also held on to a social safety net that included age pensions (introduced in 1909–10), child endowment (1941), widows' pensions (1942), funeral benefits (1943) and unemployment benefits (1945).[31] Yet in 1950 we still spent less per person on these programs than the United Kingdom, the United States or New Zealand.[32] A key reason for this was the decision in the 1930s to means-test the Australian age pension. Other countries provided benefits that were equal across the board (or which were linked to earnings, and so more generous to those at the top). Their welfare states acted like piggy banks, helping people smooth income across their lives. But from an early stage, the Australian welfare state would redistribute income from the rich to the poor. Like age pensions, the invalid and widows' pensions were means-tested. This focus on the neediest has been a key feature of Australian welfare.

The statistics on inequality in the post-war era bear out the anecdotal evidence. Looking back to Figure 4, we can see that from the 1910s to the mid-1950s, the income share of the affluent (the top 1 per cent) fell from 12 to 8 per cent. By 1980, it was below 5 per cent. In seven decades, the income share of affluent Australians had more than halved.

A similar pattern held for the opulent (the top 0.1 per cent). In the 1910s and 1920s, the opulent had about 4 per cent of household income – forty times their proportionate share. By the 1950s, this had fallen to 2 per cent, and by

1980, it was down to 1 per cent. Under the prime ministership of Malcolm Fraser, the share of income held by the top one-thousandth of Australians was only a quarter of what it had been under Billy Hughes.

The pattern is even more startling if we look at the two hundred or so all-time richest Australians. As you'll recall from Figure 2, around 30 per cent were in their peak years in the 1820s, and 20 per cent in the 1880s and 1890s. In the 1910s, about 5 per cent of all-time rich-listers were occupying the well-padded seats of Australia's exclusive clubs. But then a funny thing happened. Like the Tasmanian tiger, the Australian magnate disappeared in the 1930s. From 1940 to 1980, no one left an estate large enough to put them on the all-time rich list. For forty years, Australia was mogul-free.

William Rubinstein, who compiled the rich list, noted the near-absence of millionaires during the post-war decades. In the 1940s and 1950s, he wrote, there were only a handful of Australians worth more than £1 million. In 1955, for example, the cut-off to make the all-time rich list was £8 million. No one came close.

In this era, corporate Australia was shifting from a period of asset-owning proprietors to professional managers, but managerial salaries were yet to take off. As Donald Horne noted, 'Most business executives now were not self-made men, or inheritors of family position, but people who worked their way up through one or more business bureaucracies.'[33] Analysing the historical records of BHP ('the big Australian'), researcher Mike Pottenger and

I estimated that the BHP CEO earned fifty times as much as an average worker at the start of the twentieth century, but only fifteen times as much by the late 1940s.[34]

For society as a whole, these were prosperous decades. In the Menzies era (1949–66), real wage growth was 4 per cent a year; five times faster than it had been from 1901 to 1940.[35] For ordinary workers, the late 1950s and early 1960s saw paid annual holidays increase from one week to three.[36] By the 1960s, most Australian homes had a vacuum cleaner, a washing machine, a radio and a television. There was a fridge in 97 per cent of Australian homes in the 1960s, an appliance that most Britons, Germans and Italians did not yet possess.[37]

Australian incomes in the post-war era were rising faster at the bottom than the top. In one study, I looked at the distribution of incomes across Australian males. In an era when men were the main breadwinners, their income said a lot about how money was distributed across families. From the early 1940s to the late 1970s, I found a significant drop in male inequality.[38] To put the size of the equalisation in perspective, the reduction in inequality over these three decades was as large as the modern-day difference in inequality between Australia and the much more equal countries of Scandinavia.[39] Falling inequality among men was accompanied by a steady narrowing of the gender pay gap during this period, with the equal pay cases of 1969 and 1972 being key milestones.[40]

For Australia to make such a shift in a single generation was radical, and the change was keenly felt by those at the top of the heap. Rubinstein writes that 'so markedly different were trends among the very rich compared with those for society as a whole that the post-war period seemed to constitute, as it were, an age of affluence for everyone except the very affluent'.[41]

The social norms of this era were different. Rubinstein argues that 'most of the wealthy now eschewed conspicuous consumption and ostentatious display of riches and privilege as politically unwise and economically costly'.[42] Craig McGregor, writing in the 1960s, said that the wealthy 'feel under some pressure to be accepted by ordinary working Australians rather than the other way round'.[43] He noted a survey of the time which found that 54 per cent of Australians described themselves as 'middle class', significantly higher than the share in the United States (42 per cent) and the United Kingdom (35 per cent).[44] Visiting in 1963, Dame Edith Sitwell said, 'I am struck by something indisputably *gentle* about Australia.'[45]

One influence on the egalitarianism of the post-war decades was a romanticised notion of the bush ethos. As Russel Ward noted in 1958:

> Through the trade union movement, through such periodicals as the Sydney *Bulletin*, the *Lone Hand*, or the Queensland *Worker*, and through the work of literary men like Furphy, Lawson or Paterson, the attitudes and values of the nomad tribe were made the principal ingredient of a national *mystique*.[46]

It is invariably difficult to know whether the egalitarian spirit shapes a more equal society or the other way around. In this instance, my guess is that the man from Snowy River deserves only some of the credit. True, ours was a very equal nation in the 1950s and 1960s, but the post-war fall in inequality was not unique to Australia. Atkinson and I have also estimated top incomes for New Zealand, where we see almost precisely the same pattern.[47]

Across many advanced nations, inequality fell during the first three-quarters of the twentieth century. As universal suffrage allowed government to escape the clutches of the elites, social-democratic governments won office and implemented significant social reforms, including mass education, public healthcare, pensions, public housing and unemployment benefits. At the start of the twentieth century, Western European governments spent mostly on defence, police and justice, and accounted for less than one-tenth of the economy. By the 1970s, those governments spent substantial sums on health, education and welfare, and accounted for over two-fifths of the economy. Another important equalising factor for European nations were the two world wars, which significantly reduced the wealth shares of the richest, and shaped politics in favour of a more redistributive state.[48]

In the United Kingdom, the fall in wealth inequality over this period was especially dramatic.[49] Recall from Chapter 1 that in 1900 the richest 1 per cent of Britons owned two-thirds of all wealth. By 1980, that share was down to about one-sixth. One of the chief drivers of

Britain's wealth equalisation was the spread of home ownership. When World War I came to an end, three-quarters of Britain's housing stock was owned by private landlords. By 1981, private landlords owned only about one-tenth of properties. Other egalitarian policies implemented by the UK government after World War II included an expansion of educational opportunities, a stronger social safety net and employment policies that helped workers organise collectively for better pay and conditions.

In the United States, the 1929 share-market crash led to financial regulations that reduced the power of the financier-industrialists who had prospered in previous decades. The New Deal increased home ownership, expanded private pensions and made income taxes more progressive. President Franklin D. Roosevelt recognised that excessive wealth concentration could endanger the social compact, and that prosperity needed to be more broadly shared. The number of US millionaires almost halved between 1925 and 1950.[50] Claudia Goldin and Robert Margo have dubbed the reduction in US inequality in this period 'the Great Compression'. Across a broad range of metrics, they found that wage and income inequality fell in the United States in the post-war decades. Within workplaces, the earnings gap between skilled and unskilled workers narrowed; across occupations, incomes grew faster at the bottom than the top.[51] In the 1950s, the economist Simon Kuznets suggested that while inequality had risen in the early stage of industrialisation, it would now inexorably trend downwards in advanced nations. John Kenneth Galbraith declared that 'poverty, inequality and economic peril are of the past'.[52] By the 1970s, inequality had stayed low for so long that one economist wrote that studying it 'was like watching the grass grow'.[53]

However, we should be wary of romanticising the economy of the post-war decades. Although these were good decades for reducing inequality, discrimination against many groups was worse than it is today.[54] Thousands of talented women were shut out of the professions, many same-sex couples stayed in the closet for fear of being ostracised, and First Nations Australians were not properly counted in the census until 1967.[55] It was a time when a member of my own party could joke in parliament that 'two Wongs don't make a White', indicating that racial inequity remained alive and well.[56]

Australia was also a more closed economy. This was the era of high tariff walls (known as 'protection all round'). These trade and immigration barriers may have helped reduce poverty for the white men who constituted the bulk of the Australian labour force, but they also reduced our growth rate. Although our economy grew at a decent clip in this era, it was outpaced by most other advanced nations. From the 1950s to the 1980s, Australia grew about 1 per cent per year more slowly than the typical OECD country.[57] While we should seek to learn from the egalitarian post-war decades, it would be a mistake to try to revisit them.

≠

The spirit of the great compression is summed up in the story of Essington Lewis, the chief executive of BHP from 1921 to 1950.[58] An aggressive, hard-working man, Lewis's early tenure at BHP saw the use of 'shadow boards', which marked on the wall where each tool was meant to go and prevented workers from 'borrowing' tools for their personal use. When the Great Depression hit, he callously described it as a 'fiery furnace' which was 'necessary to put us on a proper economic basis'.[59]

And yet Lewis's personal dealings with BHP's workers were characterised by egalitarianism. Inspecting the company's steelworks in Newcastle, Whyalla and Port Kembla, he was said to be more comfortable with factory workers than engineers or clerks. During one visit, he pointed to the shadow board and asked an old hand, 'What's the magnifying glass for?' The steelworker was relaxed enough to reply, 'That's so I can see me pay.'

World War II shaped Lewis's views too. Because he was close to Prime Minister Robert Menzies, Lewis was appointed director of munitions in 1940. When John Curtin replaced Menzies, Lewis was kept in the job and came to respect the Labor leadership team. His belief in the importance of a strong central government limited his criticism of post-war economic regulation.

In 1921, Lewis was paid £4000, about twenty-four times the average wage.[60] Over the following three decades, his wage grew more slowly than that of the average factory worker. When he died in 1961, Lewis's entire wealth was valued at £98,000, about a hundred times the average annual

Australian wage at the time.[61] To put this in perspective, in 2023, BHP CEO Mike Henry earned two hundred times the average Australian full-time wage *in a single year*.[62] It is to the current era of rising inequality that I now turn.

3
The 1980s to Today – the Great Divergence

In late 2001, at the age of fifty-five, the Australian journalist Elisabeth Wynhausen decided to take leave from her job and try life as a low-wage worker. Following in the footsteps of George Orwell (*Down and Out in Paris and London*) and Barbara Ehrenreich (*Nickel and Dimed*), Wynhausen spent the best part of a year staying in budget accommodation and working at entry-level jobs.

In one job, Wynhausen moved to a country town and worked packing eggs. She earned $14 an hour in a job that started at 6 a.m., left her body aching at the end of the day, and where the smell from the nearby chook sheds was constant. Three weeks in, the manager, a millionaire several times over, came to speak to the workers. He announced that the company was selling its egg division. 'It's not all doom and gloom,' he told them – but they knew their jobs were going. Wynhausen was struck by the fact that none of the workers challenged the manager: 'seeing them standing mute in front of the boss was like seeing them stripped of all defences.'[1]

The story of Australian inequality varies according to your perspective. My maternal grandfather, Roly Stebbins, was born in a tent in 1922, and left school at age fourteen to earn money for the family. Yet broadly shared prosperity in the post-war era allowed Roly and his wife, Jean, to buy a car, build a home and raise four children into the middle class.[2] Roly lived to the age of ninety-two. For most of his life, inequality in Australia was falling. By contrast, members of Generation Y have seen inequality rise pretty much throughout their lives, with income and wealth gaps widening considerably.

One way to see this is to look at differences in earnings. Since 1975, the Australian Bureau of Statistics has surveyed employees about their salaries, allowing us to track wages at the top and bottom.[3] Figure 5 shows how wages for adult full-time workers have changed over the past four decades, with all figures expressed in 2024 dollars to adjust for inflation.

Since 1975, full-time wages for the median employee (the fiftieth percentile) have increased 47 per cent (from $61,000 to $90,000). For a worker in the tenth percentile, wages have risen only 28 per cent (from $46,000 to $58,000). For someone in the ninetieth percentile, wages have risen 74 per cent (from $92,000 to $160,000). If workers in the tenth percentile had enjoyed the same wage gains as those in the ninetieth, they would be earning an extra $21,000 a year.

Who's at the top and bottom of the distribution? Tax data suggest that among the lowest paid occupations are

Figure 5: Annual earnings (adjusting for inflation)

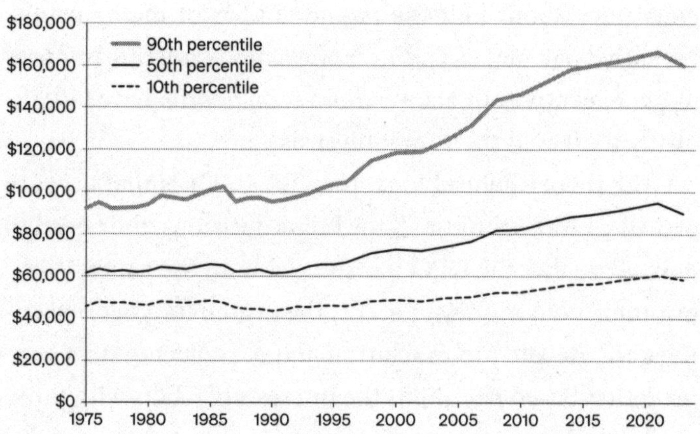

beauty salon assistants, kitchen hands, domestic cleaners, café workers, trolley collectors, vegetable pickers, pet groomers and gymnasts. Among the top paid are surgeons, financial dealers, anaesthetists, mining engineers, judges, gynaecologists and cricketers.[4]

Among top corporate executives, earnings have increased even faster. Remuneration of ASX 100 CEOs rose rapidly during the 1990s, and has continued to climb since. In 2001, the median reported pay of an ASX 100 CEO was $1.8 million (forty-seven times median full-time earnings). In 2022, it was $4.6 million (fifty-four times median earnings).[5] On a realised-pay basis, 2022 saw thirteen CEOs earn eight-figure salaries ($10 million or more).[6]

A major driver of this trend is the shift towards incentive-based pay. In the late 1980s, bonuses typically accounted for less than one-tenth of CEO pay; a decade later, they accounted for about one-third. Today, bonuses constitute about half the pay for CEOs of major firms.[7] Incentive pay makes CEO earnings more volatile. In order to get executives to accept more risk, boards have significantly increased their total rewards.

The theory behind incentives for CEOs is that because boards cannot monitor all the boss's decisions, they need to make sure that the CEO has some skin in the game. Without their own money at stake, the argument goes, executives will devote too much time to pet projects. At its best, incentive-based pay aligns the interests of CEOs with those of shareholders.

Yet too many CEO contracts overpay for good luck and over-punish for bad. Historically, CEO pay has closely tracked the overall share-market index.[8] Since no individual firm has much effect on the whole market, rewarding bosses when the entire share market rises (and penalising them when it falls) is hardly a clever strategy.[9] This has improved somewhat in recent years, with institutional shareholders paying greater attention to executive remuneration. They have been helped by a 2011 law that can prompt a spill of the board if more than a quarter of the shareholders vote against the remuneration report two years in a row. Yet companies are still reluctant to withhold bonus payments: in 2022, the typical ASX 100 CEO got more than two-thirds of their maximum bonus, and only one received zero bonus.[10]

CEO pay has also been pushed upwards by the rapid growth of our largest firms. From 1987 to 2007, the top twenty firms grew more than twice as fast as the rest of the Australian share market.[11] When two firms merge, wages typically rise in the corner offices, but not on the front desk. As the biggest got bigger, it is unsurprising that they were willing to spend more on their CEO. Economists have also pointed to the global competition for 'superstar' CEOs, an issue I will return to in the next chapter.

Higher top pay spills across to other occupations. The pay for politicians and judges isn't set by a free market, but by a Remuneration Tribunal that benchmarks salaries against what it regards as 'comparable' occupations. So these salaries are a reflection of what is happening at the top end of the labour market. Over the period from World War II until the early 1980s, salaries of federal MPs and High Court Justices grew more slowly than the pay of average workers.[12] But over the past thirty years, the pay of federal MPs has increased from twice to three times average wages, while the pay of High Court Justices has grown from five to seven times average wages.[13]

For a more complete picture of income distribution, recall Figure 4. In 1980, top income shares in Australia were at a seventy-year low. The income share of the affluent (the top 1 per cent) was below 5 per cent, while that of the opulent (the top 0.1 per cent) was around 1 per cent. Then these shares began to rise. Over the past thirty years, the affluent have almost doubled their share (to 8 per cent of household income excluding capital gains, and 10 per cent of income including capital gains), while the opulent have tripled their share (to 3 per cent of all household income excluding capital gains and 4 per cent of household income including capital gains).[14] Overall, inequality is not yet at the levels that prevailed in the 1910s, but it's close. Researchers have also shown a high degree of income persistence among the affluent.[15] If someone reports an income in the top 1 per cent, there's more than a 70 per cent chance that they will be in the top 1 per cent the following year. The persistence of top incomes rose in the mid-2000s and early 2010s. It's sticky at the top.

Like the great compression, the great divergence has also occurred in Canada, New Zealand, the United Kingdom and the United States. The difference between rising US and Australian inequality does not lie in the trend, but rather in where the nations started and finished. For example, since 1980 the income share of Australia's affluent has risen from 5 to 8 per cent, while in the United States it has increased from 10 to 21 per cent. So on this measure, Australia is almost twice as unequal as it was in 1980 – but the United States is still twice as unequal as Australia.[16] Women are significantly under-represented among high-income Australians, making up one-quarter of the top 10 per cent, one-fifth of the top 1 per cent and one-sixth of the top 0.1 per cent.[17]

One way of understanding what has happened over recent decades is to look at the distribution of economic growth across the population. The top tenth received 12 per cent of all household income gains from 1950 to 1981, but 93 per cent of the income growth from 2009 to 2019 (a higher share than in the United States or European Union during this decade).[18] Broader measures also show a rise in inequality, although the trend is not as stark as we see at the top. Review papers by experts including Peter Whiteford, Rob Bray, Roger Wilkins and Peter Saunders tend to conclude that even after accounting for the equalising effect of taxes and welfare payments, the gap between the top and the bottom grew from the early 1980s to the late 2000s.[19] (Incidentally, the welfare system has twice the equalising force of the tax system.[20])

Another way to measure inequality is to look at the share of people living on less than half the median income. This measure, known as 'relative poverty', increased in the 1980s, 1990s, 2010s and early 2020s. According to the most recent estimate, 13 per cent of Australians are in relative poverty.[21] Just as the top is accelerating away from the middle, so too is the bottom falling away from the middle. If you think of inequality as being like a foot race, everyone is still moving in the same direction, but the front runners are accelerating away from the pack, while the laggards are falling further behind. Most studies also show a rising gap in the total value of what the rich and poor consume.[22] Again, while the Australian patterns are troubling, they're less extreme than those in the United States, where real incomes for households at the bottom tenth have grown at just 1 per cent a year for the past half-century.[23]

Although earning gaps have grown for those in the labour force, Australia has a relatively high minimum wage by international standards. This means that one of the most significant contributors to inequality across households isn't how much you're paid but whether or not you work. In a household among the poorest tenth, only 18 per cent of adults are employed; in the richest tenth of households, 88 per cent of adults have a paid job. Australia's unemployment rate is low by historical standards, but joblessness has become more concentrated across neighbourhoods and families.[24]

Other measures point in the same direction. We often think of domestic servants as a feature of the past, populating nineteenth-century novels of Emily Brontë and Charles Dickens. Yet one study estimated that the servant share of the workforce, after declining for most of the twentieth century, more than doubled from the 1980s to the 1990s.[25] The super-rich employ maids, nannies, chefs and security guards. Companies have established themselves in the 'household management' industry, catering to the personnel needs of the opulent (and sometimes the affluent).[26]

Until now, I've mostly viewed the great divergence through the lens of income. But if you want to see some seriously large gaps, look not at what people take home each year, but at the total value of everything they own: their wealth. In general, the poor spend everything they earn (and then some), while the rich save significant amounts. Moreover, the poor seldom get much from their parents, while the rich can generally expect a bequest (tax-free since Australian inheritance taxes were abolished in 1979).

While you can find out about someone's income with a question or two, learning about their wealth takes more time. Think of your own case: chances are that you have a good idea of what your taxable *income* will be at the end of the year, but figuring out your *wealth* involves putting a value on assets such as a car, home and television, remembering how much you've got in investments, and subtracting debts.[27]

The most straightforward approach is to start with the largest source of wealth in the economy. Just as earnings are the biggest component of income, property is the biggest component of wealth. This means that the property market is fundamental to wealth inequality. In Chapter 1, I charted the number of days that the typical full-time employee had to work to buy a hectare of farmland (ignoring taxes). The third line of Figure 3 picks up the series in 1994, when five days' work would buy a hectare of farmland. In 2023, that number had more than tripled, to seventeen days. Measured in terms of average wages, farms are far less affordable than they were a generation ago.

But most workers aspire to buy a house, not a farm, so the more relevant comparison is between earnings and house prices. Figure 6 shows the ratio of average house prices in Sydney and Melbourne to average Australian full-time wages, starting in 1880.[28] The shape of the chart follows a similar pattern to the other inequality graphs in this book. In the late 1800s, the typical house cost around six years' earnings. This figure fell through the early decades of the twentieth century, and by the 1940s the average house cost just three years' earnings. Homes cost around four times average earnings in the 1980s, and around five times average earnings in the 1990s. But in the early 2000s, house prices began to skyrocket away from wages. By the early 2010s, the typical house was worth seven years' wages. By the early 2020s, the typical house was worth eleven years' wages, a ratio almost three time as high as it was in the 1980s. Measured in terms of housing affordability, Australian inequality is worse than at any time in recorded history.

Figure 6: How many years' earnings does the average house cost?

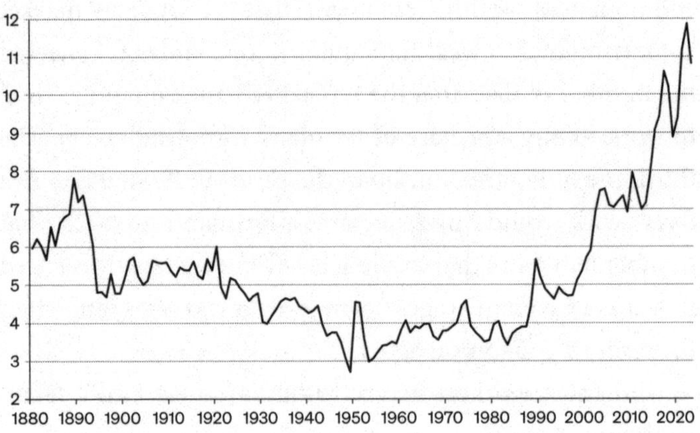

Housing affordability is a key driver of home ownership. In the 1940s and 1950s, Australian home ownership rose rapidly. But since the 1980s, the share of adults who own their home has declined. This drop has been particularly marked for younger people. In 1981, the home-ownership rate among people aged twenty-five to thirty-four was 61 per cent. In 2021, it was 43 per cent. One study looked at how long it took to save for a 20 per cent deposit. In the early 1990s, it took the average Australian about seven years to save such a deposit. By the early 2020s, it took almost twelve years. Many young people see themselves as 'forever renters'.[29]

A more comprehensive analysis of wealth points in the same direction. In collaboration with economist Pamela Katic, I drew together data from wealth surveys and inheritance tax records to estimate long-run wealth inequality.[30] Our estimates include not only houses, but cars, shares and bank deposits.[31] Our results suggest a similar pattern to that for top income shares, but with even more dramatic trends. From 1915 to 1953, the wealth share of the affluent fell from 34 to 15 per cent, and by 1978 it had fallen still further, to 7 per cent.[32] Over the following decades, the wealth share of the affluent rose steadily.

The wealth share of the opulent has followed a similar trajectory. They had 13 per cent of wealth in 1915, 5 per cent of wealth in 1953 and 2 per cent in 1978. In the past generation, the wealth share of the opulent has risen. As was shown in Figure 1, changes at the very top affect the whole population. If we rank everyone by their wealth and divide them into five equal-sized groups, we see that the shares of the bottom four groups have shrunk since the 1960s, while that of the top group has grown.

Thanks to information from rich lists, we don't have to stop at the top one-thousandth of wealth-holders. We can look at how many on the current lists would qualify for the all-time rich list.[33] As you'll recall from Figure 2, no one on the 1983, 1984 or 1985 rich lists made the cut – continuing a more than four-decade absence of magnates. Then, in 1986, three Australians made the all-time rich list. The mogul was back. Within a few years, tycoons like Kerry Packer and Alan Bond were making headlines. The spirit of the time was captured by the man who protested against one of Bond's coastal developments by changing his name to 'Fast Bucks'.[34]

While some of the names on the Australian rich list changed, the wealth of the super-rich kept growing, largely unaffected by events such as the 1987 stock-market crash.[35] In the 1990s, the top ranks of the list were populated by men such as Frank Lowy, Richard Pratt and Harry Triguboff. In the 2000s, we saw the rise of Andrew Forrest, Clive Palmer, Ivan Glasenberg and, most spectacularly, Gina Rinehart.

In 2024, the cut-off to enter the top-200 rich list was $718 million, and wealth holdings increase rapidly from that point. Oilman John Paul Getty once said: 'If you can count your money, you don't have a billion dollars.' Australia now has 150 billionaires. Twenty-three people on the 2024 rich list would qualify for the all-time Australian rich list, down from twenty-eight in 2022.

The share of Australian wealth held by the super-rich is steadily rising. Figure 7 shows the share of household wealth held by the top 0.001 per cent of adults (two hundred people in recent years) and the share held by the top 0.0001 per cent of adults (twenty people in recent years).[36] From 1983 to 2024, the top 0.001 per cent increased their share of Australian household wealth more than fivefold, from 0.7 per cent to 4.2 per cent. Over the same period, the top 0.0001 per cent increased their share of national income from 0.2 per cent to 2.1 per cent: more than a ninefold increase.

The top twenty Australians now have twice as much wealth as the bottom two million households.[37]

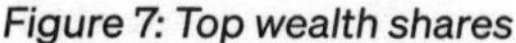

Figure 7: Top wealth shares

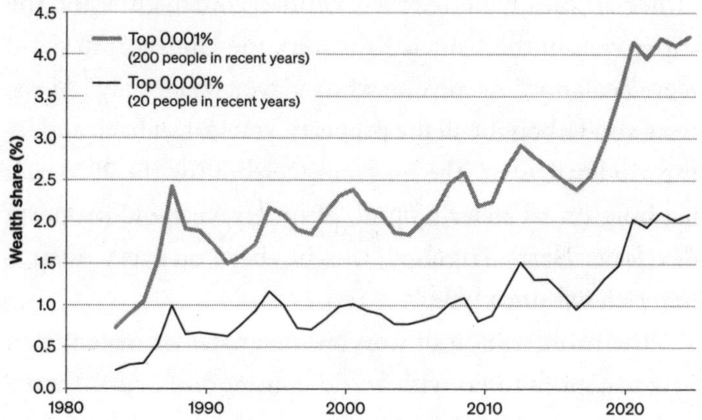

In the Introduction to this book, I discussed the question of whether those on the rich list earned their money from working harder and smarter than everyone else, or through super-normal profits (known by economists as 'rents'). To analyse this question, Lachlan Hotchin and I studied the industries in which Australian rich-listers made their fortunes. We then compared the degree of market concentration in those industries with the average degree of market concentration across the economy.[38] We began by looking at top wealth-holders in 1990 and concluded that they had tended to make their money in industries where market concentration was higher than in the economy as a whole. We then looked at the data for 2020 and found that the problem had become more pronounced. The industries that made top wealth-holders rich tend to be sectors such as iron ore mining, paper manufacturing and television broadcasting, where markets are especially concentrated. Other studies have reached similar conclusions for the super-rich in the United Kingdom, the United States and New Zealand.[39] As anyone who's played Monopoly knows, once you've bought all the property, you just sit back and let the money flow in. The magazine celebrating the 2023 rich list bore on its cover a photo of ninety-year-old property developer Harry Triguboff, who has been on every Australian rich list since 1983.[40]

The proliferation of iron ore magnates on recent rich lists has more to do with world commodity prices than a sudden surge of hard work and innovation by mining entrepreneurs. As I noted in the Introduction, the difference in wealth between Rinehart and her father, Lang Hancock, is hard to explain as anything other than Rinehart enjoying greater 'economic rents'. And while the late Richard Pratt's business savvy was often lauded as the reason for his success, his cardboard box business was found in 2007 to have operated what the Federal Court called 'the most serious cartel case to come before the Court in the thirty-plus years in which price fixing has been prohibited by statute'.[41]

The impact of rising wealth inequality has been felt by many Australians. A survey in 2000 asked if the distribution of wealth was fairer, less fair, or about the same as in 1990. Eleven per cent said it was fairer, 30 per cent said no difference, and 59 per cent said it was less fair.[42] Asked in

2023 whether they felt that 'The gap between rich and poor is too great and should be reduced', 74 per cent agreed while only 7 per cent disagreed.[43]

I once presented some of these findings at the University of the Third Age. In the question-and-answer session, a white-haired man asked, 'What do they spend it on? I mean, if you gave me a million dollars a year, I wouldn't know what to do with it.'

I appreciated the questioner's asceticism, but assured him that if he were to find himself with a seven-figure income, he would quickly discover new ways to spend the money. Matching the rise in top incomes over recent decades, there is now a plethora of ways to part the super-rich from their cash.

For a start, there are luxury homes. With only a fixed amount of waterfront land, it is no surprise that the price of harbourside property has soared as inequality has risen. For example, the median house price on Wolseley Road in Point Piper is $24 million. There are at least fifteen streets in Australia where the typical home sells for over $10 million.[44] As well as water views, top-end homes can have granite benchtops and ironbark floorboards; they can also feature customised home theatres, indoor waterslides, rock climbing walls, and infrared saunas.[45]

Now it's time to think about how you'll get to and from work. Perhaps you could start with a Porsche 911 Turbo or Maserati MC20, each costing around half a million dollars? From 2011 to 2023, Porsche sales in Australia quadrupled, after strong growth the previous decade.[46] Or there's the million-dollar carbon-fibre Lamborghini Aventador SVJ, which goes from 0 to 100 kilometres per hour in 2.8 seconds (the same rate of acceleration as if it were to fall off a cliff) and consumes over 17 litres of fuel every 100 kilometres.[47]

Another option is to take to the skies. A basic Robinson helicopter starts at around half a million dollars, but if you want something that's faster, quieter and more comfortable, you can spend over $5 million on upmarket brands such as Eurocopter.[48] Since the mid-1990s, the number of helicopters in Australia has tripled (prompting an attempt to operate a floating helipad in Sydney harbour).[49] At the start of the millennium, superyachts (craft measuring 24 metres or longer) were virtually unknown in Australia. Now, there are around 120 superyachts owned by Australians. Sydney, Melbourne, Cairns and the Gold Coast have all undergone marina upgrades to cater for superyachts.[50]

If you want to travel interstate or overseas, you're probably looking for a private plane. While Cessnas are the most common make of private aircraft, they're just the entry-level choice for the super-rich. The Bombardier Global Express 7500, which can fly nonstop from Australia to the continental United States, costs around US$75 million. At least four Australian billionaires own one.[51] In the past two decades, the global fleet of private jets has more than doubled, and according to one report, Australia has the fourth-largest market in the world for private jets.[52]

If you're interested in politics, why not buy a billboard advertisement? Over the past decade, Mineralogy, the mining company owned by billionaire Clive Palmer, has donated over $200 million to Palmer's United Australia Party. Prior to the 2019 election, Palmer's advertising expenditure topped that of Labor and the Coalition combined, and even exceeded the advertising spending of Coles, Toyota or McDonald's.[53]

Wondering what to consume? According to the connoisseurs, one of the greatest vintages for Penfolds Grange Hermitage is the 1971, a bottle of which will cost you about $2000, or about $40 a sip. Incidentally, that bottle has increased in price at four times the rate of average earnings: a reflection of the increased demand for high-end commodities.[54] Or if your tastes tend to the illicit, you might consider cocaine – what Robin Williams once described as 'God's way of telling you that you are making too much money'. Cocaine is most prevalent in affluent neighbourhoods, and the share of Australians who used cocaine in the past twelve months has risen eightfold, from 0.5 per cent in 1993 to 4.2 per cent in 2019.[55]

When it comes to holidays, I'm indebted to Jacquie Hayes, who for some years wrote an unselfconscious column called 'First Class' for the *Australian Financial Review*. Flying back from Paris, she laments that all the seats at the front of the plane are occupied, and asks, 'Is it really worth flying first class on Qantas any more?'[56] She thinks more highly of Emirates, appreciating their in-flight showers ('as I crossed the Tasman Sea the other day at 40,000 feet, naked and standing on a heated bathroom floor'), but tut-tutting when the airline substitutes the 2003 Dom Perignon for the 2000 vintage (a wine 'lacking the seductiveness of the advertised 2000').[57] In case you haven't flown first class lately, a return flight to Europe costs around $20,000 to $30,000.

Among her many overseas jaunts, Hayes describes helicopter rides in Hong Kong and yacht trips in Auckland. She suggests readers book their place on the Virgin Galactic Space Flight (currently retailing at US$600,000).[58] A keyword that crops up often in her writing is 'private': she takes private lessons, invests in private equity and stays in the private sections of top-rated hotels.[59] Some private treatments sound tempting, while others are distinctly odd. After staying in the 'private ski beach' section of an exclusive Utah resort, she writes: 'I don't think I'll get used to pulling my ski boots on or off myself – the St Regis ski valet staff take care of that here.'[60]

Yearning for privacy, Hayes asks why there isn't a proper private members' club in Australia, akin to those in London and Hong Kong, where women don diamonds and waiters allegedly charge based on the quality of guests' wristwatches. She sighs: 'Annual subscriptions may only be a couple of grand a year, yet the very best of this breed of private club are synonymous with sophistication, exclusivity and unapologetic snobbery.'[61]

Hayes' tastes surely aren't unusual for the super-rich. If they were, the *Australian Financial Review* wouldn't have given her a column. Her desire for exclusivity points to the way in which the super-rich are constantly comparing themselves with each other. *What are all these people doing in first class? How do I get the best dress at the Melbourne Cup?*

Can we create a club that keeps out the single-figure millionaires, and only lets in those worth at least $10 million? These status games are costly to play because 'the best' is often scarce. There are only so many Picassos, private islands and landing bays for private planes.[62]

While average incomes in Australia have been steadily rising, we should not forget about the extent of deprivation at the bottom end. In 2022, 12 per cent of Australians could not afford a week's holiday away from home each year, 7 per cent could not afford at least $500 in savings for an emergency, 4 per cent could not afford dental treatment if they needed it and 2 per cent could not afford presents for immediate family members or close friends at least once a year. Each year, eight out of a thousand children were subject to a case of substantiated abuse or neglect.[63] For Australia's most disadvantaged, some worry that the 'fair go' has gone.

≠

In 1995, one social researcher reported: 'The more Australians think about their increasingly competitive society, the more they ... reflect wistfully on the possibility that the ideal of Australia as an egalitarian society is being challenged (and may already have disappeared).' As a focus group participant put it:

> The haves and have-nots are now very distinct groups, these days. In the fifties and sixties, the people seemed to be more equal ... Now you have a lot of these rich

> households ... contrasted with those families who are struggling along on welfare.[64]

The great divergence is over a generation old, having begun around 1980. During this period, most people at the bottom and middle have become better off, but the gains have been more modest than at the top. As Midnight Oil's Peter Garrett presciently put it, 'the rich get richer, the poor get the picture'.[65] Measured in terms of consumption, income or wealth, the last generation has seen the rich outpace the poor. In the next chapter, I set about trying to understand the factors that caused the great convergence and the great divergence. What drives inequality?

4
Drivers of Inequality

The story so far. After more than a century of fluctuating inequality (from English settlement to World War I), inequality in Australia fell for about half a century. In the past generation, the gap between rich and poor has widened again. Internationally, Australia's level of inequality now ranks around the middle of the pack. For example, a recent comparison finds that Australia has the seventeenth-highest level of inequality among thirty-eight advanced nations.[1]

If all you knew about Australia was that we were a rich country that spoke English, that's about where you'd expect to find us. As Figure 8 shows, there are clear global patterns of inequality. Latin American countries tend to be among the most unequal, followed by English-speaking nations (with the United States leading that group) and Mediterranean countries. Northern Europe tends to be more equal again, and the most equal of all are the Scandinavian and Eastern European nations.

Figure 8: Comparing income inequality across advanced countries

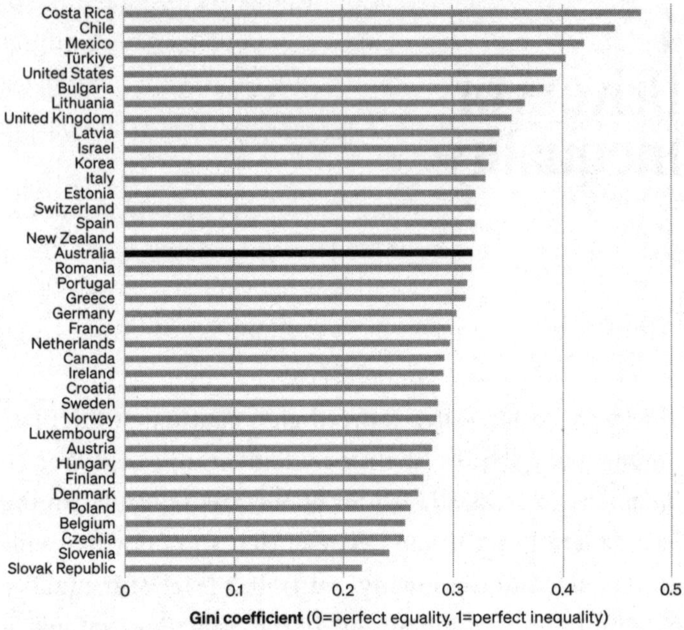

Costa Rica
Chile
Mexico
Türkiye
United States
Bulgaria
Lithuania
United Kingdom
Latvia
Israel
Korea
Italy
Estonia
Switzerland
Spain
New Zealand
Australia
Romania
Portugal
Greece
Germany
France
Netherlands
Canada
Ireland
Croatia
Sweden
Norway
Luxembourg
Austria
Hungary
Finland
Denmark
Poland
Belgium
Czechia
Slovenia
Slovak Republic

0 0.1 0.2 0.3 0.4 0.5

Gini coefficient (0=perfect equality, 1=perfect inequality)

In this chapter, I will explore the big factors that drive differences across countries and changes over time. These include technology and globalisation (which have combined to create 'superstar' workers), union membership, taxation and education.

Technology and Globalisation

Imagine you want to be filthy rich. What activity might earn massive returns in a capitalist economy? For a start, you will need to be able to do something that no one else can do and which other people want to buy. For example, you might make great tools, be an exceptional leader, provide valued entertainment or heal the sick. At any time or place in history, you would be rewarded by your community for having these skills. But to move from being rich to filthy rich, you need a way of magnifying your skills to reach a larger audience.

That's where technology and globalisation come in.[2] By allowing talented workers to affect more people, technology and globalisation turn those who would once have been mere 'stars' into what economists call 'superstars'. Because the world has experienced a rapid period of technological improvement and global connectedness, we have more superstars today than ever before.[3]

The economist Sherwin Rosen explains superstar labour markets by contrasting Elizabeth Billington, an opera star from the early 1800s, with Luciano Pavarotti, who died in 2007.[4] While Billington sang to a full house in Covent Garden and Drury Lane, she performed in the era before recording, and so was unable to reach a wider audience. Consequently, Billington earned around £10,000 a year (about AUD$800,000), while Pavarotti earned at least $20 million annually.[5] Recording technology acted as a force multiplier: not only adding another income source, but also allowing Pavarotti to reach a global audience where Billington could reach only a local one.

More recent data has shown that globalisation and technological change have led to more inequality in the music industry. Looking at concert revenue, one study found that in 1981, the top 1 per cent of musicians (such as U2, Bruce

Springsteen and the Rolling Stones) garnered 26 per cent of the total.[6] By 2017, that figure had more than doubled, with 60 per cent of concert revenue going to the top 1 per cent of musicians (which included Justin Bieber, Beyoncé and Coldplay). In 1964, the priciest tickets to see the Beatles in Australia cost $3.70 ($63 adjusted for inflation). In 2024, the most expensive tickets to see Taylor Swift in Australia cost $1250.[7]

The same 'winner takes all' dynamic can also be seen in the movie industry. Over the past generation, the top tenth of Hollywood movies have steadily increased their share of total revenue: 62 per cent in 1982, 67 per cent in 1992, 68 per cent in 2002, 76 per cent in 2012 and 90 per cent in 2022.[8] In 2021, a single movie, *Spider-Man: No Way Home*, accounted for one-eighth of all US cinema revenue. According to the *New York Times* film critic Janet Maslin, the shift towards mass-market blockbusters began with the success of *Jaws* in 1975.[9] Over the ensuing decades, producers increasingly eschewed niche artistic films that characterised the pre-*Jaws* era (for example, *Mean Streets, Chinatown, The Conversation*) in favour of mass-market blockbusters (for example, *Beverley Hills Cop, Terminator, Alien*). As smash-hit movies replaced hidden gems, the earnings of top actors entered the stratosphere. In 2023, Jason Statham, Leonardo DiCaprio, Jennifer Aniston, Matt Damon, Ryan Gosling, Tom Cruise, Margot Robbie and Adam Sandler each earned over US$40 million.[10]

In Australia, technology has significantly advantaged those at the top. Email and videoconferencing have boosted the productivity of office professionals, but barely changed the daily tasks of hairdressers and childcare workers. As I noted in the last chapter, our biggest firms have grown larger, which means that those who run them have taken on more responsibility (and been handsomely remunerated for doing so), while the rest of the workers haven't seen their pay packets grow commensurately. At the same time, Australia is increasingly connected to the rest of the world, with professional service firms serving the Asia-Pacific and executive recruitment panels searching globally for talent.

One industry that has been affected by technology and globalisation is my former profession of law. In the 1980s, many firms were city-based and the fax machine was the hottest technology around. Consequently, the best lawyer in a large Sydney firm would service the most profitable Sydney clients. By the 1990s, national partnerships were common: airfares had fallen and email and mobile phones allowed rapid communication, meaning that the top Sydney partners were increasingly looking after the top Australian clients. Since the 2000s, with the rise of international partnerships and the ubiquity of videoconferencing, a senior Sydney partner is likely to be working for the firm's top Asia-Pacific clients. So it's no surprise that a superstar Sydney lawyer is earning more than ever before.

Research by Michael Coelli and Jeff Borland points to what they call the 'routinisation hypothesis'.[11] Over the past five decades, job growth has been weak or non-existent in occupations involving routine tasks, such as basic clerical and production jobs. In these occupations, computers and robots have increasingly taken over from people. By contrast, there has been strong job growth in occupations involving the kinds of non-routine cognitive work typically done by professionals, technical experts and managers. Not only have computers struggled to supplant professionals in these roles; technological developments have often benefited those professionals (as we saw in the law example above). It remains unclear whether new artificial-intelligence tools will change this pattern or simply serve to make professionals and managers more productive. Among lower-paid occupations, recent decades have seen solid job growth in occupations involving non-routine manual work, such as personal care, food preparation, cleaning and security services. Robot waiters and robot security guards remain rare.

The globalisation of Australia's CEO market is another example of superstar labour markets at work. One of the first overseas CEOs was Bob Joss, brought in to head Westpac in 1993 on an annual salary nearly as large as those of the other three major bank CEOs combined.[12] Since then, Australians have become accustomed to overseas-born CEOs such as Ahmed Fahour (Australia Post), Ross McEwan (NAB), Sol Trujillo (Telstra) and Alan Joyce (Qantas). We may get better talent as a result, but one of the consequences of doing a worldwide search is that we now pay the global price for CEOs – even if a local gets the job. Moreover, because firms want 'the best' CEO, there's a tendency to overpay.[13] Mathematically, half of all CEOs must be paid less than the median. Yet only about one-twentieth of firms said that they would give their CEO a remuneration package below the median.[14] The remuneration of chief executives at Australia's 100 largest listed firms is around a hundred times average earnings, while remuneration for CEOs at the top 100 US firms is almost three hundred times average US earnings.[15]

This globalisation of professional labour markets is a particular advantage for English speakers. If you look at the income share of the top 1 per cent, you'll see that it's risen much more steeply in English-speaking countries, such as Australia, Canada, New Zealand, the United Kingdom and the United States, than in non-English-speaking countries, such as France, Germany, Japan, the Netherlands and Switzerland.[16] If you're an English-speaking CEO, globalisation just magnified your job options. But if you're a German-speaking CEO, your options haven't changed much. Indeed, one Canadian study found that the increase in top earnings had been much smaller in the predominantly French-speaking province of Quebec.[17] While a top English-speaking accountant in Toronto could readily move south to take a job in the United States, globalisation hadn't done much for her French-speaking counterpart in Montreal.

Unions

A powerful force for equality in Australia has been the union movement. Unions foster equality in different ways. One is that they can tip the scales towards workers as a whole by increasing the wage bill and reducing profits. This applies particularly for firms that enjoy a monopoly position. An extreme example is a one-company town. When employees have no choice about where to work, the firm can pay them a pittance. Forming a union means that workers have collective power, because they can now threaten to stop work if their pay demands aren't met.

Another way that unions reduce pay gaps is by pushing harder to raise the earnings of the lowest paid. Unions have typically done this by advocating fixed-dollar pay increases rather than percentage increases. For example, $50 a week is a 10 per cent wage rise for someone with weekly earnings of $500, but a mere 2 per cent wage rise for someone on $2500.[18] Unions have also sought to reduce wages at the top, for example by advocating curbs on executive pay.[19] These redistributive wage demands are an expression of the democratic structure of unions.

Unions also attempt to influence redistribution through the political system. In Australia, the most significant manifestation of this was the creation in 1891 of the Australian Labor Party, which formed government at the federal level just thirteen years later. Labor still retains a strong union link, with half the delegates to our national conference representing their union. Internationally, 'labourist' parties such as the ALP tend to be more in favour of redistribution than social-democratic parties like the US Democratic Party.

From as early as 1834, when the Tolpuddle Martyrs were transported to New South Wales for trying to form a union, Australia had a strong association with collective bargaining. The oldest unions were formed in the 1830s. In 1856, Melbourne building workers won an eight-hour day. Subsequent decades saw the formation of unions representing miners, seamen and tailoresses, and the 1890s shearers' strikes over wages and employment rules. A universal forty-hour working week was finally won in 1947, and four weeks' annual leave came in 1974.[20] Unions today are pressing for pay equity – making the case that workers in female-dominated industries have been systematically underpaid.

Figure 9 plots union membership since 1891, combining multiple estimates to form a consistent series.[21] (For a discussion of the factors that caused the collapse in union membership, see my 2010 book, *Disconnected*.) On the same chart, I have shown the share of income (including capital gains) held by the top 1 per cent.

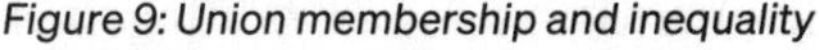
Figure 9: Union membership and inequality

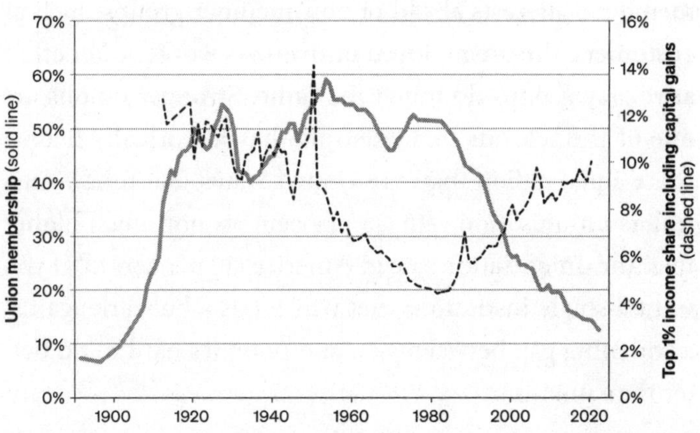

The results show a moderately strong inverse relationship between inequality and union membership. Around 1980, the low point of Australian inequality, one in two workers were members of a union. The most recent survey, in 2022, was conducted in a much more unequal Australia, and found that the union-membership rate had fallen to just one in eight.

Graphs aside, the academic evidence on this point is quite clear. A fall in union membership has been shown to be responsible for a significant portion of the rise in US inequality in the 1980s, and for most of the difference in inequality between the United States and United Kingdom.[22] One study for Australia suggested that up to one-third of the change in inequality during the 1980s and 1990s was due to the collapse of unions.[23]

Economists are fond of complaining about the role of unions. They are sometimes criticised for advocating their members' interests ahead of non-member groups, such as customers, the unemployed or overseas workers. Yet other advocacy groups do much the same. Stronger unions are one of the reasons that Australia has historically been a more equal nation than the United States. But today, Australia's unionisation rate (13 per cent) is not much higher than the unionisation rate in America (10 per cent).[24] If you want a single institution that will act as a bulwark against a widening gap between rich and poor, it's hard to do better than unions.

Taxation

Another important factor affecting inequality is the tax system. For the first hundred years after British settlement, Australia was almost solely reliant on import taxes (tariffs) for government revenue. It took a long time before Australia saw progressive taxes such as inheritance taxes (first levied in 1868), land taxes (1878) and income taxes (1880): each partly a response to rising economic inequality.[25] But even in 1901, the various tiers of government together raised five times as much from tariffs as from taxes on inheritance, land and income put together.[26] A 1904 reform pamphlet described the taxation system of the time as 'inequitable, unequal and cumbersome'.[27]

With the outbreak of World War I, Australia imposed federal inheritance taxes (in 1914) and federal income taxes (in 1915). Yet total revenue from state and federal income taxes remained below that from tariffs until 1941, when World War II prompted the federal government to turn income tax from an elite into a mass tax.

Figure 10 shows two lines: the top income tax rate (the highest rate paid by anyone in the country) and the income tax rate paid by a typical person in the top 1 per cent. Obtaining the schedules for recent decades is easy, since only the federal government levies income taxes. It's a bit more complicated for the early decades of the twentieth century, since each state had its own income tax and they were fond of adding extra levies and surcharges.[28]

When I first looked at Figure 10, two things immediately struck me. The first was that for most of the twentieth century, the top tax rate was higher than the tax rate paid by a typical member of the top 1 per cent. For example, in 1921, the top tax rate was 45 per cent, but this rate applied only to a tiny fraction of the population. The typical tax rate paid by the top 1 per cent was 11 per cent. Only since 1979 has the top tax bracket come down low enough that most people in the top 1 per cent paid the top tax rate (from that point on, the two lines sit on top of each other.)

Figure 10: Top income tax rates

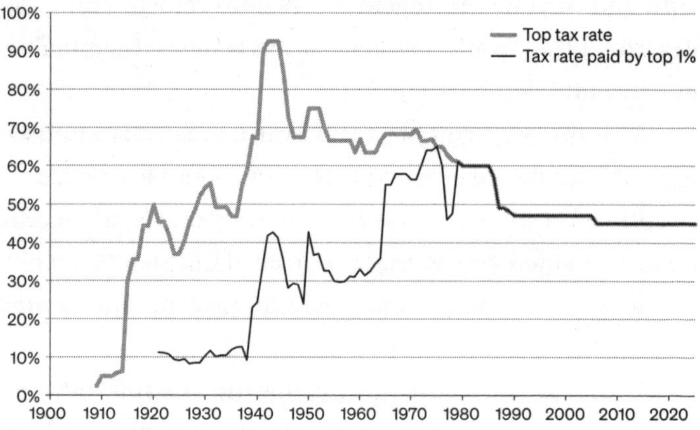

Second, the chart shows a strong inverted-U shape, which neatly mirrors the trajectory of the top 1 per cent share. The top tax rate peaked in the years from 1942 to 1944, when it was a whopping 93 per cent (the United States and United Kingdom went higher still, at 94 per cent and 97.5 per cent respectively). The highest rate paid by the top 1 per cent peaked at 65 per cent in 1975. Since then, the top tax rate (and the marginal rate paid by the top 1 per cent) has steadily fallen: from 60 per cent in the early 1980s, to 47 per cent in the 1990s and to 45 per cent today.[29]

Some of Australia's tax cuts have been accompanied by measures to expand the tax base. For example, the government expanded the capital gains tax in 1985 and began to tax fringe benefits in 1986.[30] Many services (and some goods) that had previously been untaxed were covered by the goods and services tax, which came into effect in 2000. Yet there were also measures in the other direction, such as the scrapping of state and federal inheritance taxes in the late 1970s, and the decision in 1999 to halve the capital gains tax on assets held for more than a year.[31] For most high-income earners, a generation of reforms to 'broaden the base and lower the rate' has seen a reduction in their average tax rate.

Australia's cuts to the top tax rate in the past generation mirrored a global trend, with many advanced countries reducing their highest income tax rates in the 1980s and 1990s. Advocates of these tax cuts correctly point out that very high taxes can reduce entrepreneurial effort and discourage saving. But the cuts have also directly contributed to the rise in inequality. Lower taxes increase top wage earnings by providing an incentive to take on additional work, and they increase capital earnings by allowing investors to reinvest a greater share. So cuts to the top tax rate have the effect of increasing top incomes. Based on research with Sir Tony Atkinson, I estimate that one-third of the rise in top incomes over recent decades is due to cuts in top tax rates.[32]

Education

One of the most intriguing explanations of what drives inequality was put forward by the Harvard academic supercouple Claudia Goldin and Larry Katz.[33] They suggest that we should think of inequality as a 'race' between technology and education. In eras when technological advances outpace schooling attainment, the gap between rich and poor widens. But in times when the quantity and quality of education increases, so too does equality.

In the United States, Goldin and Katz argue the first seventy-five years of the twentieth century saw rapid educational advances. The 'high-school movement' saw a boom in school construction during the inter-war era. By the mid-1930s, it was normal for a young person living in the north of the United States to complete ten years of schooling, a standard not achieved in Australia until the mid-1960s. In the 1950s in the United States, there was a boom in university attendance (a boom that did not hit Australia until the 1980s). Yet in the past generation, US educational attainment has stagnated while technology has continued to advance. Technology is winning the race, and US inequality is skyrocketing.

For Australia, our big educational booms have been the primary-schooling movement of the late nineteenth century (which increased adult literacy from under 75 per cent to over 90 per cent), a significant increase in high-school completion rates from the 1960s to the 1980s, and a rise in university completions in the past generation.[34] Yet over the past decade, educational gaps have grown. At the top end, the share of twenty-five to thirty-four-year-olds with a bachelor's degree has risen (from 37 per cent in 2014 to 45 per cent in 2023). But other young people are struggling. School attendance rates have dropped, and the share of young people completing high school has fallen from 82 per cent in 2012 to 79 per cent in 2023.[35] Many other advanced countries have higher levels of educational attainment than Australia.[36]

Historically, periods of educational stagnation are not unusual.[37] If we estimate average years of education (including school and university) among the Australian working-age population, we can see that they rose by only about a year from 1920 to 1960.[38] But from 1960 to 1980, they rose by three years.[39] Australia's education boom arrived at least a generation after the US boom and continued into the twenty-first century. The technological shock of the computer revolution did increase Australian inequality, but by less than it would have done if we had not also continued to raise the quantity of education at the same time.

It's easy to see why education is the great equaliser when we look at the individual benefit. Someone who completes Year 12 is 22 per cent more likely to have a job than someone who drops out in Year 9.[40] For those with a job, high-school completion raises annual earnings by 44 per cent (compared with leaving school in Year 9). Compared with someone who finished Year 12 but has no post-school qualifications, a diploma boosts earnings by 11 per cent, while a bachelor's degree boosts earnings by 41 per cent (equating to more than a million dollars over a lifetime).[41] Despite significant increases in education, the wage returns have stayed constant over recent decades, debunking claims that we're becoming 'overeducated'.[42] Measures to boost education levels – such as raising the minimum school leaving age and increasing the number of university places – are likely to have an equalising effect.

Yet while the quantity of Australian education has risen significantly, test scores have failed to improve. University of Melbourne researcher Chris Ryan and I found that the results of Australian secondary students on an international maths test had fallen from 1964 to 2003, and test scores on a separate literacy test had worsened from 1975 to 1998.[43]

Recent evidence tells a mostly troubling tale. The OECD's international PISA exam – which tests how well students can apply what they've learned in school to real-world situations – has been testing Australian fifteen-year-olds since the early 2000s. Over that time, average reading, maths and science scores have fallen. By 2022, the decline in reading and maths was equivalent to a full year of learning, meaning that fifteen-year-olds were scoring at the same level as fourteen-year-olds two decades earlier.[44] Australia's own NAPLAN tests, which test students in five different subjects at four different year levels, mostly showed no improvement from 2008 to 2022.[45] The only hint of optimism comes from an international maths and science test (TIMSS), which showed improvements in performance from 1995 to 2019.[46]

Figure 11: Test score inequality and earnings inequality

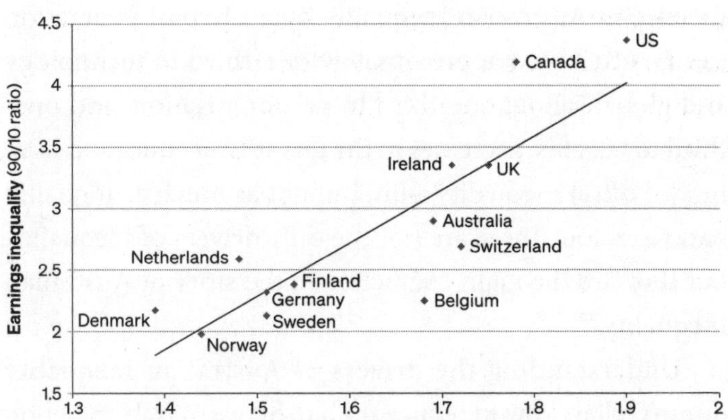

So while Australians are staying at school longer than previous generations, today's secondary students are performing no better than their parents did (and on some tests, worse). This means that in the 'race' between education and technology, education is hopping on one leg.

We should also be concerned about the relatively large gap between high- and low-performing students. As Figure 11 demonstrates, countries with larger test-score gaps also have larger wage gaps. While the effects could run in either direction, these findings are yet another reason to redouble our national efforts to improve education for the most disadvantaged. Disturbingly, the gap in reading scores between advantaged and disadvantaged students in Year 3 widened from 1.4 years in 2008 to 2.3 years in 2022.[47]

≠

Putting the effects in this chapter together, I estimate that the rise in Australian inequality over the past generation can be attributed approximately one-third to technology and globalisation, one-third to de-unionisation, and one-third to tax cuts. Increases in the quantity of education have helped offset inequality a bit, but not as much as if quality had risen too. These are not the only drivers of inequality, but they are the main characters in the story of Australian inequality.[48]

Understanding the drivers of Australian inequality doesn't tell us how to reduce the gap between rich and poor. Raising tariffs to 'protect' local industry has a superficial appeal until you think about how much more it would cost to produce an Australian-made television. Capping CEO salaries might sound tempting until you recall reports from the 1980s and 1990s that bemoaned the low quality of Australian managers.[49] Globalisation is here to stay. The same is true of technology. Few of us would give up the internet, with the global connectedness that accompanies it. From the English Luddites who smashed automated looms in the 1810s to the Australian shearers who attempted to block the introduction of wide combs in the 1980s, history is littered with examples of people who tried and failed to stop technological innovation.

The best we can do is to teach people to swim in rough waters. Increasing the quantity and quality of education becomes vital as technology advances. For example, a mechanic who lacks the skills to replace an onboard computer is destined to be the one washing the wheels in a few decades' time. Schools, universities and companies should help people master the new artificial intelligence tools, so that apps such as ChatGPT make workers more productive – rather than redundant.

We also need to keep inequality firmly in mind when devising taxation and industrial relations policies. Few people would argue for reinstating the 60 per cent top income tax rate that prevailed a generation ago, which surely deterred some entrepreneurs from starting down the rocky road towards creating their own businesses. It's rare to hear anyone argue for a return to 'closed shops': workplaces where union membership is compulsory. But we need to be aware that further reductions in top tax rates and union membership are likely to cause inequality to rise.

Having looked at the drivers of inequality, the next question is: does it matter? Is inequality really such a bad thing, or might it even have some benefits?

5
Consequences of Inequality

Let's take a moment to look at inequality on the sporting field by comparing one of the most unequal contests – English Premier League football – with one of the most equal – the Australian Football League. Of the thirty EPL championships between 1994 and 2023, two teams, Manchester United and Manchester City, have won nineteen.[1] In the same period, no AFL team has won more than four premierships. Over these three decades, only seven different teams won the EPL championships, while fourteen different teams have won the AFL premiership.

There are simple structural reasons for this difference. English football operates much like feudalism. The money from television rights is shared out according to each team's finishing position, with the top-ranked teams getting the most. Players are signed by scouts, who search the globe for promising players. A recent report put Manchester City's salary bill at £423 million (around AUD$800 million).[2] The AFL is a great deal more egalitarian. Television revenue goes to the league, which shares it out evenly among the teams. Players enter the game via a draft, in which lower ranked teams get first pick of promising players. And a team's total salary bill is capped at $16 million (rising to $18 million in 2025). Teams such as the Geelong Cats have argued that the AFL should do even more redistribution, but everyone admits there is more equalisation in the AFL than in English football.[3]

Supporters of the more unequal game might point to the innovations that English football engenders. With such vast resources, Manchester United and Manchester City are at the cutting edge in their use of technology, development of game strategies, medical treatment of injured players and selection of new recruits. These phenomenally rich clubs are able to pioneer techniques that are then adopted by other teams.

But inequality comes at a cost. Economists describe the Australian Football League as having more 'competitive balance' than the English Premier League, meaning that you're more likely to see an upset at the AFL. The main reason to make any sport more equal is so that it becomes interesting to watch. English football these days tends to be tiresomely predictable.

It wasn't always like this. Prior to the 1970s, when Australian sports began instituting changes to increase 'competitive balance', EPL football was the more unpredictable sport. From the 1880s to the 1960s, no EPL team won more than 10 per cent of all championships, while in the AFL (then known as the Victorian Football League),

Collingwood won 18 per cent of all premierships. For that period, the list of all the different teams that became EPL champions is twice as long as the list of all the different teams that became AFL premiers.[4]

Yet in recent decades, the two leagues have radically diverged. English football has become increasingly unequal, while the AFL has been fairly equal. In the past thirty years, twice as many teams have become AFL premiers as EPL champions. Just three teams – Manchester United, Manchester City and Chelsea – account for 80 per cent of the EPL champions in the modern era.[5]

Rugby League, too, has instituted reforms to improve competitive balance. As we have seen, the game emerged as a response to Rugby Union's refusal to allow player payments. Yet despite its egalitarian beginnings, the early decades of League showed the kind of fixed hierarchy that would have made a baron blush. From 1925 to 1929, the winners were South Sydney, South Sydney, South Sydney, South Sydney and South Sydney. In the post-war era, St George won eleven premierships in a row. Yet in the 1970s, League began to get more competitive balance. Players could move more readily across teams. New clubs were encouraged to enter the competition, with the number of teams almost doubling from the 1970s to the 1990s. In the 1990s, a salary cap was instituted. Despite the Penrith Panthers' recent run, League is a much more fluid competition today than it was before those reforms.[6]

Inequality not only has costs *across* sporting teams; even *within* teams, larger gaps can reduce performance.

One study looked at the significant rise in salary inequality in US major league baseball.[7] It found that teams with large gaps between the best and worst paid players underperformed those with more equal wage distributions.

In this chapter, I will discuss why inequality matters, addressing head-on the criticism that the gap between rich and poor shouldn't concern policymakers. This puts me at odds with some famous economists. For example, Robert Lucas argued that 'of the tendencies that are harmful to sound economics, the most seductive, and in my opinion, the most poisonous, is to focus on questions of distribution'. Martin Feldstein believed that 'there is nothing wrong with an increase in wellbeing of the wealthy or with an increase in inequality that results [solely] from a rise in high incomes'.[8]

One of the arguments most often made by such critics is that discussions of inequality distract from the more important problem of improving outcomes for the truly disadvantaged. Why worry about the gap between the rich and the rest, the argument goes, when we should be concerned with the wellbeing of the poor?

The problem with this argument is that while we might be able to set an appropriate poverty line for a decade or two, rising incomes for the middle class will eventually change our notions of what poverty means. For example, the seven-shilling minimum wage that was seen as reasonable in the 1907 Harvester judgment would be regarded as grossly inadequate today. The least affluent Australians are richer than half the world's population, but we wouldn't tell someone in Blacktown to compare themselves with the poor in Bangladesh.[9] Even definitions of homelessness depend on what is classed as 'inadequate housing'. By today's definition, most nineteenth-century Australians would be regarded as homeless.[10] You can't define poverty without thinking about what's normal in a society.[11] As the British historian Richard Tawney neatly noted: 'what thoughtful rich people call the problem of poverty, thoughtful poor people call with equal justice a problem of riches'.[12]

The interrelationship between the wellbeing of the rich and poor was recognised by the grandfather of modern economics, Adam Smith, who argued:

> This disposition to admire, and almost to worship, the rich and the powerful, and to despise, or, at least, to neglect persons of poor and mean condition ... is ... the great and most universal cause of the corruption of our moral sentiments.[13]

To Smith, it was only fair that everyone should get a share of the national wealth, that schooling be free, and taxation be progressive.[14] A focus on inequality has marked the writings of many Nobel laureates in economics, including Claudia Goldin, David Card, Angus Deaton, Simon Kuznets, Amartya Sen, Joseph Stiglitz and Paul Krugman.[15]

Broadly speaking, arguments about inequality fall into two groups. The first are 'instrumental' arguments: inequality matters because it affects something else that you care about (such as growth or mobility). The second are 'intrinsic' arguments: inequality matters inherently.

Let's start with the instrumental arguments, beginning with the question: do unequal countries grow faster or slower? Christopher Jencks (Harvard), Dan Andrews (OECD) and I took data for the past half-century and looked at whether initial inequality predicted economic growth. We found an effect, although not in the direction I had expected. Our study concluded that countries with higher income inequality experienced *more rapid* economic growth.[16]

One reason for this might be that inequality spurs entrepreneurs to take risks. Starting a business can often be exhausting and risky. If your start-up idea means working sixteen-hour days and taking out a second mortgage on your home, you're probably more likely to take a shot if the rewards of success are very high. Another reason might be that today's rich provide tomorrow's start-up capital. You can see this happening in places like Silicon Valley and Tel Aviv, where the super-rich often invest in new ventures.[17]

Yet while the effects of inequality on growth are positive, 'trickle-down' works slowly. Viewed from the standpoint of the bottom 90 per cent, we found that it took over a decade for them to get enough economic growth to make up for having a smaller income share. Put another way, it takes quite a while for the pie to grow enough to make up for the fact that the poor have received a smaller slice.

Another instrumental reason to care about inequality is its impact on social mobility. Although the data isn't clear-cut, it looks as though in countries with larger income gaps, the accident of your birth tends to determine where you end up. In the next chapter, I will discuss what we know about intergenerational mobility in Australia, and the suggestive evidence that inequality makes it harder for someone to move from adversity to abundance. Although inequality is often justified on the basis of mobility, it looks as though there isn't much of a trade-off between the two. Instead, countries tend to get the best or worst of both worlds: equal societies are mobile, while unequal societies are also immobile.

A third instrumental reason to be concerned about inequality is its impact on democracy. As we saw in the Introduction, the rich are more likely than the poor to engage in political activity (such as contacting government officials or signing petitions). But there is also reason to think that rising inequality may skew political outcomes towards the interests of the most affluent. As the Republican Party boss Mark Hanna said of US politics in the Gilded Age: 'There are two things that are important in politics. The first is money, and I can't remember the second.' Studies have found that US senators' voting behaviour is very strongly related to the opinions of their richest constituents, modestly related to those of middle-income constituents, and unrelated to the views of low-income constituents.[18] Contrary to Plato's fear that the poor would wield too much power in an unequal democracy, the reverse seems to be closer to the mark.[19]

Inequality can also affect political outcomes by shaping our notion of the common good. Democracy does not require perfect equality, but a strong democracy does depend on a society with enough equality that people 'bump up' against those who are different from them. Without a modicum of social mixing, shared interests can become subservient to self-interest. When the most affluent use different hospitals and schools, travel solely by private transport and live among those in their own income bracket, they may lose touch with the need for a strong safety net to protect the most disadvantaged. It works the other way, too. If the poor are cut off from the rich, they may cease to understand how hard you have to work to create a successful business. (In the United States, leisure time has become increasingly unequally distributed – while the rich have a larger share of the money, the poor have a larger share of the leisure time.[20])

Looking beyond growth, mobility and democracy, others have claimed that inequality – as distinct from, say, poverty – worsens social outcomes such as health and crime. Yet on closer inspection, such claims turn out to be fragile. Inequality does many things, but its effects on life expectancy and homicide are small or non-existent. I'll spare you the details here, but the interested reader can find them at the end of the chapter.

Let's sum up the instrumental arguments about inequality. It is modestly good for growth, although trickle-down is very slow. Based on the available evidence, inequality is probably bad for mobility and democracy. And inequality doesn't appear to have much impact on health and crime.

Now let's turn to the intrinsic arguments. In the Introduction, I mentioned the notion of the 'veil of ignorance', devised by the philosopher John Rawls.[21] His great insight was to imagine how people would think about inequality if they did not know where in the pecking order they would end up. Put yourself in the position of a baby that's about to be born: before you leave the womb, you have no idea whether your family lives in a shack or a mansion. Given that ignorance, what kind of income distribution would you choose?

Rawls' conclusion was that from behind the veil, people would tolerate differences only if their effect was to make the poor better off. Put another way, you would only accept a smaller share if it would increase the total size of the pie. This means that you probably wouldn't choose perfect equality, since that would be a world that didn't reward effort. On the other hand, viewed from behind the veil of ignorance, extreme inequality would look as unattractive as putting all your income on one number of the roulette wheel. The ideal would be something in between.

In choosing a society with fair redistribution, we would likely have in mind the fact that our economic success is significantly shaped by factors we cannot control.[22] For example, the genetic lottery shapes our intelligence, health and looks – all factors that affect earnings. Children who have the luck to be first born have certain advantages, but that doesn't make them any more meritorious than their siblings. Luck also shapes how our talents are valued. If I'd been born into a competitive hunting society, my poor eyesight and light build would have made me a bad spear-thrower and a lousy fighter, but that wouldn't have made me any less deserving. So too a plain-spoken factory worker is of equal intrinsic worth today as he was a generation ago, even though there is now less demand for his skills. Luck affects not only what we're born with, but also whether our particular talents are rewarded by the society we join.

The veil of ignorance makes us think about justice and fairness without regard to our own attributes. Each of us needs to ask the question: what kind of a society would I want if there was an equal chance that I might be born weak or strong, male or female, with rich or poor parents, able-bodied or with a disability, Indigenous or non-Indigenous? Thinking about the world through the veil always makes me feel a little more vulnerable. My guess is that if you were faced with the prospect of starting life with myriad disadvantages, you'd probably opt for a relatively equal society.

This sense of egalitarianism reflects what Lester Thurow termed 'the income distribution as a public good'.[23] Anyone who thinks that economics is about maximising money rather than maximising wellbeing hasn't gotten past first-year university. In maximising wellbeing, inequality matters – because a dollar brings more happiness to a poor person than to a rich person. One analysis asked people to rate their happiness on a zero to ten scale, and looked at how much money was required to move them up by one point. They found that to buy the same increase in happiness cost $6000 for the poorest households, but $100,000 for the richest.[24] This is one reason redistribution makes sense – because taxing a millionaire to make sure a pauper doesn't become homeless has the effect of increasing aggregate wellbeing.

Even setting aside Rawls' veil of ignorance, there are good reasons to think that we might want to curb excessive inequality. As I'll discuss below, a mounting body of evidence tells us that humans feel a palpable discomfort at high levels of inequality. My sons are constantly benchmarking against one another. When Sebastian, my eldest, was aged six, I asked him whether he'd prefer that he and his four-year-old brother, Theodore, both got one biscuit, or he got two and Theodore got three. Without hesitation, he replied: 'I'd prefer one each.' Puzzled, I pushed Sebastian a little to find out why. 'Because it would make me sad if Theo had more than me,' came the reply.

This sentiment isn't confined to children. A survey asked US respondents whether they would prefer a world in which they had an annual income of $50,000 and others earned $25,000; or a world in which they had twice as much ($100,000) but others had four times as much ($200,000).[25] Half of those surveyed preferred to be poorer (with an income of $50,000 rather than $100,000) so long as it meant being at the top of the heap rather than the bottom. Changing the subject matter from income to other attributes (such as education or attractiveness) yielded a similar result: relativities mattered at least as much as absolutes.

In a famous economics experiment called the 'ultimatum game', the first player chooses how she would like $100 divided between her and another person.[26] The second player can either accept that split, or decide that both players will get nothing. If all people cared about was being better off, then the second player should accept the division when he gets anything at all. So if the first player proposes to keep $99 and hand over $1, a second player who doesn't care about inequality should accept. Yet in thousands of settings it has been shown that many people have a cut-off around $25, below which they'd rather get nothing than receive a share that they regard as miserly. It offends our dignity – our sense of justice.

In another economics game, players were given an option to spend $1 of their own money to reduce another player's earnings by $3.[27] Depending on our political views, we might call this 'egalitarianism', 'taxation' or 'punishment'. Regardless of the name, two-thirds of players chose to penalise another, with their targets typically being the richest players. In this game, greater equality came at a price, but most players were willing to pay it.[28] This is consistent with a large literature in psychology showing that people prefer to barrack for underdogs over favourites.[29]

Admittedly, these economics games are conducted in a laboratory, which may cause people to behave differently. John List, an economist who is sceptical about how much the ultimatum game can tell us about real-world behaviour, pointedly observes: 'What is puzzling is that neither I nor any of my family of friends (or their families and friends) have ever received an anonymous envelope stuffed with cash.'[30]

But you don't have to rely on laboratory experiments. One US study compared individuals with the same income who lived in high- and low-income neighbourhoods.[31] It turned out that as their neighbours' incomes rose, an individual's happiness fell. Another study encouraged staff at a large public university to go online and check out their co-workers' salaries.[32] The effect was to reduce job satisfaction among workers who earned less than those around them. A cross-country analysis finds that people in more unequal places tend to be less happy with their lives, an effect that holds for both rich and poor respondents.[33] Other research reaches similar conclusions.[34]

John Stuart Mill once noted, 'men do not desire to be rich, but richer than other men'.[35] He may have been overstating things, but relativities are practically important if people are competing for 'positional goods', such as a home in a desirable suburb, a place in a top university or a sought-after job. In such cases, rising top incomes may lead to an 'expenditure cascade', as those in the middle have to spend more to stay in the race.[36] When inequality is modest, a young person can happily wear a $200 outfit to a job interview. But if top incomes rise, they may feel a need to buy a $1000 outfit to compete. Similarly, the rise in cosmetic surgery (one in twenty Australians has had at least one procedure) is driven by the desire to meet a rising social standard.[37] If we feel obliged to spend more on clothes, homes and plastic surgery, then we can end up in a 'status race' that looks a lot like an arms race. As any football fan knows, once everyone gets to their feet, you have to stand up too if you want to keep watching the game. Similarly, if people's spending is based not on their own desires but the need to keep up with the Joneses, the whole thing ends up being socially wasteful.

≠

In the early 1300s, Venice was one of the richest cities on the planet.[38] A trading hub, its success owed a great deal to the ability to bring together the money of established financiers and the ideas of new entrepreneurs. The *colleganza* – akin to a company in today's capitalist economies – allowed risk-sharing and encouraged businessmen to venture trading expeditions.

Then, in 1315, Venice's social structure changed. The elites published the *Libro d'Oro* – a register of the nobility, comprising a tiny minority of all Venetians. Only those whose names were listed in the book could participate in key decisions. What had been an open society became increasingly closed. The *colleganza* was banned. For the next two centuries, Venice's population steadily shrank. What had been a successful open society became a failed experiment in established privilege.

The lesson of Venice's rise and fall shows how entrenching privilege can ultimately harm a society. Those who published the *Libro d'Oro* made Venice more unequal. That had instrumental costs, as the society became less mobile and less democratic. It also grew more slowly (suggesting that my academic findings about growth may not hold under conditions of extreme inequity). But there were surely also intrinsic arguments against what Venetians called *La Serrata* (the closure). From behind the veil of ignorance, would anyone have chosen to live in a society where those not on the list became second-class citizens?

At the other extreme, few of us behind the veil of ignorance would choose perfect equality. One reason is that it wouldn't be very interesting. The French artist Francis Picabia put it nicely when he noted: 'Nature is unfair? So much the better, inequality is the only bearable thing, the monotony of equality can only lead us to boredom.' This monotony was on full display in the Soviet Union during the 1960s and 1970s, when most citizens were assigned an apartment, had few consumer goods to choose from and could not travel outside the country.

Like other communist societies, the Soviet Union tried to put into practice the Marxist principle: 'from each according to their ability, to each according to their need'. What it found was that by entirely breaking the link between what an individual puts in and what they get back, massive damage was done to total economic output. Most people ended up with a fairly equal slice of a small and unappetising pie.

As the English philosopher Jeremy Bentham noted two centuries ago, 'Perfect equality is a chimera – all we can do is to diminish inequality.'[39] As you'll see in Chapter 7, that's the view Australians take today: few desire perfect equality, but most want smaller earnings gaps and a more equal distribution of wealth.

So inequality is about getting the balance right. Indeed, if I'd been writing this book in 1980, when the top 1 per cent share was at a seventy-year low, the top tax rate was 60 per cent and half the workforce was in a union, I doubt I would have been perturbed by Australia's level of inequality. As many economists did at the time, I might have pointed out that our high tariffs and insular culture were leading to sluggish firms and few entrepreneurs. The central economic problem of 1980 wasn't inequality; it was the closed economy.

I even have mixed feelings about inequality at home. I gave the example above of my eldest son, Sebastian, who once told me that he'd prefer that he and his brother Theodore get one biscuit apiece, rather than Sebastian getting two and Theodore getting three. On the one hand, I love that my sons are thinking about fairness, but it can also seem an infuriating waste of time to a busy parent. 'Don't worry about him,' I want to say, 'just focus on your own share!'

When I mentioned to a friend that my wife was pregnant with our third child, she surprised me by suggesting that one benefit of having three children is that we'd have fewer squabbles over who gets what. 'With two, they constantly benchmark against each other,' she said. 'With three, they don't compare as much.' So one benefit of having three children is that your kids spend less time worrying about equality. Even Labor MPs like me sometimes get sick of talking about fairness.

Until now, this book has focused on the gap between rich and poor at a single point in time. We've looked at inequality in earnings, total income and wealth. In each case, it's as though we've taken a photo of the society and compared everyone's positions. This has the advantage of being straightforward, but it misses the changes that take place over time. Life is more like a video than a photo. In the next chapter, I will focus on an issue that's intimately related to inequality: social mobility. How much change do we see from one generation to the next, what factors drive it, and how is it linked to inequality?

Technical Note: What Inequality Doesn't Do

When I began researching the effects of inequality, I expected to find large negative impacts everywhere I looked. Believing that most English-speaking countries had grown too unequal, I expected that the adverse effects of this would show up in a host of measures. But the more I looked at the data, the less certain I became that inequality was an unmitigated evil. As I have argued in this chapter, inequality appears to be good for growth and to have no substantial effects on health or crime, and perhaps to have adverse effects on social mobility and democracy.

This is a considerably more mixed bag than some other studies have found. For example, Richard Wilkinson and Kate Pickett argue that if the United Kingdom became as equal as Scandinavia, everyone would live a year longer, mental illness would be halved, teen birth rates would fall by two-thirds, homicide rates would fall by three-quarters and everyone could get seven extra weeks' holiday a year.[40] This is a heady concoction, but I can't convince myself to swallow it. The closer you get to Wilkinson and Pickett's results, the more fragile they appear.[41] Part of the problem is that they're looking at a snapshot in time rather than changes over time. Another difficulty is that their results are often driven by one or two countries (place your thumb over what looks like the most influential dot on a scatter plot, and an apparent relationship frequently disappears).[42]

To see the problem, take the case of health. As we saw in the Introduction, there is a strong relationship between an individual's income and their health. The poor have fewer teeth, experience more pain and even live for fewer years. But while a person's own income is a powerful predictor of health outcomes, there's little evidence that the poor get sicker when the rich get richer.[43] The more careful one is with the data, the less convincing is the claim that rising incomes at the top reduce the health of those at the bottom. If inequality were bad for your health, you would expect to see the biggest health improvements in the countries that had not experienced a rise in inequality. But during the last two decades of the twentieth century, improvements in life expectancy were similar in countries saw a substantial rise in inequality (such as Australia and the United Kingdom) and those where inequality stayed static (such as France and Switzerland). The impact of inequality on health is either small or non-existent.

A similar story holds for crime. In recent decades, some of the most significant reductions in violent crime have occurred in countries where inequality has risen. From the early 1990s to the early 2020s, Australia's homicide rate halved. The United States had witnessed almost as large a reduction.[44] In both countries, the gap between rich and poor widened over this period. We don't yet understand all the factors that drive crime, but it doesn't look as though inequality is a major contributor.

One reason that social scientists have been able to get into a methodological battle over the effects of inequality on health, growth and crime is that the data are reasonably good. By contrast, measures of social mobility are notoriously imprecise, and it's difficult to agree on appropriate ways to measure degrees of democracy. Because of this, my conclusions on these outcomes are more cautious. Over coming decades, I expect that researchers will steadily accumulate better evidence on social mobility and democracy, which I'll incorporate into future editions of this book, changing my conclusions if necessary.

6
Mobility

Isabel and her mother heard the shot when her father took his own life. He was twenty-one years old, her mother was nineteen and Isabel was only five months old. When Isabel was nine, she overheard that he had died by suicide rather than in an accident as she'd been told. For years, she blamed herself for her father's death.

After her father's death, Isabel mostly lived with her grandparents. They took care of eleven children, living in a small three-bedroom weatherboard house. The six boys slept in a shed out the back, with the girls in the two bedrooms inside.

When Isabel was three years old, her mother remarried and they moved into public housing. Then a half-brother was born and the family moved into their own home in a low-income neighbourhood. Isabel remembers a mother who was still growing up, and meals of Coca-Cola, chocolate and chips. She told me, 'You'd be surprised how many chips you can get for a couple of dollars, and they fill you up on a cold night.'

When Isabel was eleven, her mother divorced her second husband. Shortly afterwards, the bank called in the mortgage, and Isabel and her mother were back with the grandparents. Only this time, she shared a bedroom with her half-brother rather than her cousins.

Isabel was fifteen when her mother married her third husband. On the upside, her new stepfather was a builder, so was able to build them a house. On the downside, he was a compulsive gambler whose debts caused them to lose the house.

At twenty-two, Isabel fell pregnant to her boyfriend and decided to have the baby. She hadn't counted on his drug problem getting worse, and that the stress of the baby would lead him to become violent. When he hit her, Isabel walked out. At twenty-two, two decades after her father's suicide, she was a single mother with her own daughter.

Isabel isn't her real name, but the reason I've chosen to tell her story is because of where she's ended up. Today, Isabel is a senior figure in the federal parliament. Few people there know what she went through growing up, but she often thinks about it when she's having a hard day at work. It puts the little things into perspective, she told me.

In this chapter, I will discuss the issue of intergenerational mobility and some of the barriers to moving from poverty to prosperity (or vice versa). When we talk about inequality, we refer to the gap between rich and poor at one point in time. Intergenerational mobility is a different concept, measuring how easy it is for each generation to move up or down the economic ladder. When people say, 'The apple doesn't fall far from the tree,' they're describing a society in which children grow up to earn a similar income to their parents. Conversely, 'Anyone can make it' describes a society in which parental background is no barrier to what a child can grow up to achieve.

By the end of the chapter, I hope I will have persuaded you that mobility matters, and that it can be tough to move from the most disadvantaged neighbourhood to the most affluent. But the reason I chose to start with Isabel's story is to emphasise that we should never give up on anyone, or be gulled into thinking that demographics is destiny. Concerns about the difficulty of moving up the pecking order shouldn't ever lead us to think that a particular individual cannot make it.

Australian society prides itself on being one where people can easily move from one social class to another. Perhaps the best example is Samuel Terry, the Manchester thief transported in 1801 for stealing stockings. By the time of his death in 1838, Terry's wealth exceeded 3 per cent of the colony's total income.[1]

Writing in the 1960s, Craig McGregor argued:

> There is not so much difference between the way the different classes speak, the way they dress or the schools they went to ... The lack of widespread extremes in social differentiation makes it easy for class-jumpers to 'pass'.[2]

In the same decade, Donald Horne wrote:

> There are no possibilities in Australia of determining status by simple inspection. You can't place a man in a social scale by listening to his accent or what he talks about or by looking at his clothes or observing his manners.[3]

But even in that period, there was evidence that children tended to follow in their parents' footsteps. A survey of school-leavers in 1959–1960 found that many boys entered their fathers' occupations, including 61 per cent of farmers' sons, 38 per cent of skilled tradesmen's sons, and 36 per cent of sons of university-educated fathers. What McGregor called 'class-jumpers' did exist, but they were perhaps not as prevalent as popular wisdom suggested.

One way that economists measure social mobility is by looking at 'intergenerational elasticity'. This boils a society's level of mobility down to a single number, which asks the question: if a father's income is 10 per cent higher than average, what do we expect his son to earn when he reaches the same age? (Historical comparisons look at men because women have traditionally had lower employment rates.) In a very mobile society, a father's earnings would be unrelated to his son's wage, so the number will be small. Conversely, in a very static society, a father's earnings will have a large impact on his son's earnings. If a 10 per cent increase in fathers' earnings had zero impact on sons', the society would be perfectly mobile. If a 10 per cent increase in fathers' earnings led to a 10 per cent increase in sons', it would be entirely static, with no class-jumping whatsoever.

In a 2007 study, I estimated the relationship between the earnings of Australian fathers and sons.[4] My research found that for every additional 10 per cent that a father earns, his son's earnings rise by about 2½ per cent. This is larger than the effect in Scandinavian nations (where the 10 per cent increase pushes up sons' earnings by 1–2 per cent), but smaller than the effect in the United States (where it raises sons' earnings by 4–6 per cent). This indicates that the effect of parental background on a child's life chances is about twice as large in the United States as it is in Australia. Comparing the Australian and US results, my study found that this is particularly due to the persistence of poverty in the United States: someone born into the bottom fifth of the income distribution has half as good a chance of making it into the top fifth in the United States as they would in Australia.

Another way to think about the level of social mobility in Australia is to compare the intergenerational transmission of income with that of a characteristic that we know to be affected by genes: height. For every 10 per cent increase in a father's height, his son's height goes up 5 per cent. Take a moment to think about a few father–son pairs that you know. My guess is that not many of them involve very short sons and tall fathers (or vice-versa). In the United States, the heritability of income is similar to the heritability of height.[5] But in Australia, income is only about half as heritable as height. In Scandinavia, the hereditability of income is smaller still.

In past decade, better data has enabled Australian researchers to produce several excellent studies on intergenerational mobility.[6] The finding that Australia is a more socially mobile country than the United States holds up across multiple datasets and approaches (and is true for wealth mobility too). We have also learned more about the factors that drive Australian intergenerational mobility, with researchers pointing to the role of segregation, education and family structure.[7] Researchers have also looked at the question of absolute mobility, asking, 'Are we richer than our parents were?' It turns out that while four-fifths of baby boomers had higher real incomes than their parents, this figure has fallen to two-thirds for recent generations.[8]

In this chapter, I will argue that the life chances of advantaged and disadvantaged children stem from three big differences: money, parents and time. Disadvantaged children are typically raised by fewer parents, in households that are poorer, and with less parental time spent on them.

Whatever your political views, I expect there's a part of this chapter that will make you shift uneasily in your seat. Many conservatives take the view that the gap between rich and poor doesn't matter, because every child can make it if they try hard enough. Unfortunately, the evidence I will present throws a bucket of cold water over this view.

On the other hand, many progressives don't like to talk about the effects of parenting on social mobility. We may spend hours reading *Harry Potter* to our children, but we tend to cringe at the idea that what we're doing is transmitting privilege across generations. There's something comforting about the thought that all parents are just muddling through. And yet it turns out that not all family structures and parenting styles are equally effective – at least as measured by children's academic and economic outcomes. But before I gingerly pick my way through the thorny ground of families and parenting, let's talk about money.

At the start of this chapter, I distinguished inequality (the income gaps that exist in a society) from mobility (the ease of class-jumping). It's now time to look at how these two concepts are related to one another. Are unequal societies the most fluid? Or are the nations with large gaps between rich and poor also those where people occupy the same class from birth to death?

The question isn't merely of academic interest. In a survey covering several advanced countries (including Britain, the United States and Germany, though not Australia), the vast majority agreed with the statement: 'It's fair if people have more money and wealth, but only if there are equal opportunities.'[9] Many people are willing to bear high inequality – but only if it comes with high mobility.

Alas, the empirical evidence seems to point the other way. Writing in 2009, OECD researcher Dan Andrews and I looked at inequality and social mobility in ten nations. We found evidence that nations with more inequality in the mid-1970s were less socially mobile in the ensuing quarter-century.[10] A few years later, the US economist Alan Krueger presented more evidence for this pattern, which he memorably tagged 'the Great Gatsby Curve'.[11] Recently, the Canadian economist Miles Corak has compiled evidence from sixteen advanced countries that shows the same pattern.[12]

If high inequality entrenches poverty and plutocracy across generations, it will damage something that many of us hold sacred.[13] If inequality makes us a more static society, then the rich list will increasingly be populated by those with inherited wealth rather than the self-made. One way to see this is to look at the pattern of inheritances. Figure 12 shows the share of inheritances received by people in different wealth deciles. In 2022, the poorest half of households received just 10 per cent of inheritances, while the richest tenth of households received 43 per cent of all inheritances. With property prices at record highs, inheritances are likely to further increase Australian inequality.[14]

Figure 12: Share of inheritances by household wealth decile

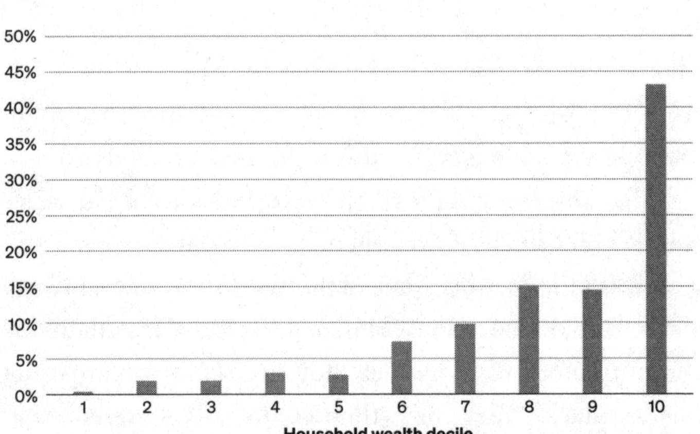

The fact that more inequality leads to less social mobility is most shocking to those in the United States.[15] Deep in the American psyche is the notion that theirs is a nation where anyone can make it. Regaling the Democratic Convention in 2004 with his extraordinary life story, Barack Obama claimed that 'in no other country on earth is my story even possible'.[16] Yet he acknowledged, as president, that 'it is harder today for a child born here in America to improve her station in life than it is for children in most of our wealthy allies'. If anything, it has become harder for an American to move from penury to plenty.[17]

In theory, a society could be unequal (with a large gap between rich and poor), but mobile (with lots of class-jumping). In practice, this doesn't tend to happen. Societies with a large gulf separating the haves and have-nots are generally those in which few people escape the circumstances of their birth. To see this, think back to the ladder analogy in the Introduction. If inequality measures the gaps between the rungs, then intergenerational mobility measures how easy it is to climb up or down. If the rungs move wider apart, the ladder becomes harder for someone to climb. In a very unequal society, you are likely to stay on your birth rung.

Now let's talk families. The debate over the role that family structure plays in perpetuating poverty over generations has a long lineage. One of the most famous treatments of the issue was a 1965 report issued by the US assistant secretary of labor, Daniel Patrick Moynihan. Moynihan's focus was on Black Americans (then commonly referred to as 'Negroes').[18] The Moynihan Report argued:

> The gap between the Negro and most other groups in American society is widening. The fundamental problem, in which this is most clearly the case, is that of family structure. The evidence – not final, but powerfully persuasive – is that the Negro family in the urban ghettos is crumbling. A middle-class group has managed to save itself, but for vast numbers of the unskilled, poorly educated city working class the fabric of conventional social relationships has all but disintegrated. There are indications that the situation may have been arrested in the past few years, but the general post-war trend is unmistakable. So long as this situation persists, the cycle of poverty and disadvantage will continue to repeat itself.
>
> The thesis of this paper is that these events, in combination, confront the nation with a new kind of problem. Measures that have worked in the past, or would work for most groups in the present, will not work here. A national effort is required that will give a unity of purpose to the many activities of the Federal government in this area, directed to a new kind of national goal: the establishment of a stable Negro family structure.

Moynihan argued that high levels of single parenthood among Black Americans were partly a legacy of slavery (a system in which 30 per cent of slave children were sold before their tenth birthday), as well as poverty, unemployment and low wages in the modern era.[19]

Upon its release, the Moynihan Report was attacked by many on the progressive left, including the Black American leaders Al Sharpton and Jesse Jackson. Moynihan was accused of stereotyping black men, focusing too much on behaviour and giving racism a free pass. The title of one book that criticised Moynihan was *Blaming the Victim*: it was a term that quickly entered common usage.[20]

Nearly half a century after the Moynihan Report, the share of Black American children born to unmarried parents has risen from one-quarter to three-quarters. And yet it's easy to see why Moynihan's diagnosis still rankles. Black American men have seen their incarceration rates soar and their wages flatline, so it's harder than ever to be a good dad. And the millions of Black American women who are struggling to make it as sole mothers have enough on their plates without being told that their failure to marry is hurting their children.

The same is true of the debate about lone parenthood in Australia. Nothing has made me more in awe of lone parents than having children. When our boys are ill, my wife and I sometimes shake our heads and ask, 'How do lone parents do it?' From speaking with constituents who are raising children on their own, I know what enormous sacrifices they make. Yet while the topic is uncomfortable, there's no getting away from the simple fact that it's easier to raise a child with two adults than one. So if we are to understand how and why patterns of disadvantage are replicated across generations, it's important to think about the role of family structure.

Initially, I'll focus on lone parenthood, since talking about 'marriage' has a moral sting that can inflame the debate. Later, though, I'll return to thinking about why marriage might matter.

The first thing to note is that the share of Australian children in lone-parent households has approximately doubled over the past generation. On recent figures, 22 per cent of children live in such households, up from about 10 per cent in the late 1970s.[21] In public debates, commentators often attribute the rising share of children living in lone-parent households to the increase in the divorce rate, but the statistics don't bear this out. While the introduction of no-fault divorce in 1975 led to a surge of divorces in the following year, the current divorce rate is only slightly higher than it was before the legislation passed.[22] Instead, the rise in lone-parent households is mostly driven by lower partnering rates.

If the rise in lone parenthood was spread equally across advantaged and disadvantaged families, it might not have much impact on social mobility. But that's not the pattern that researchers have observed. In general, children from poor families are less likely to live with both parents than children from well-off families.

One way that this can be seen is by looking at First Nations children, a traditionally disadvantaged group. Across Australia, almost half of First Nations children live in single-parent families, considerably higher than the national average.[23] Given that First Nations children face a host of other barriers – from lower-quality public services to poor housing to racism – it is troubling that so many live in lone-parent households.

Another marker of low socioeconomic status is lower levels of education. Is the decline in partnering happening across all education groups, or is it particularly concentrated among those with less education? To test this, I compared children whose parents both had a university degree with children where neither parent had a university degree. I then asked the question: were children with university-educated parents more or less likely to be living with both parents at the age of fourteen?[24]

For children born in the 1940s and 1950s, children of university-educated parents were actually less likely to be living with both parents than children of non-university-educated parents. Among baby boomers where neither parent had a university degree, around 87 per cent were living with both parents. Among baby boomers whose parents both had a university degree, around 83 per cent were living with both parents. For children born in the 1960s and early 1970s, the share living with both parents at age fourteen did not differ according to parental education.

Then from the late 1970s birth cohort onwards, the lines diverged. Those in Generation Y were more likely to be living with both parents in their teenage years if their parents had university degrees. The same was true for Millennials. Among Generation Z (those born from the mid-1990s onwards) the gap has widened to over 20 percentage points. Children born in 2007 have an 88 per cent change of living with both parents if their parents have university degrees, but a 66 per cent chance of living with both parents if neither parent has a university degree. Since the 1940s, children of university-educated parents have become slightly more likely to be living with both parents, while children of non-university-educated parents became much less likely to be living with both parents.[25]

Figure 13: Share of children living with both parents at age fourteen

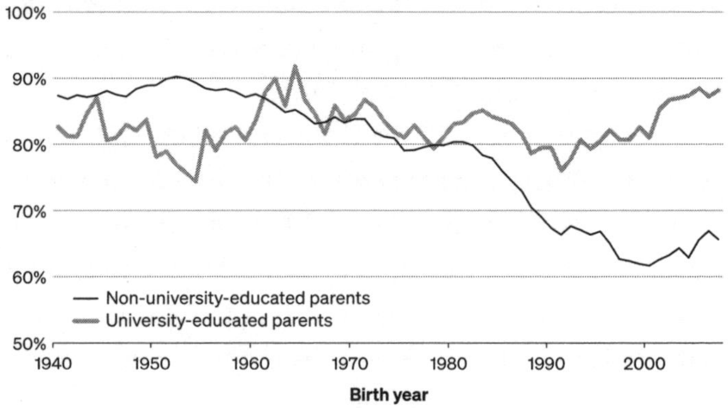

The result is that First Nations children and those in less-educated households are more likely to be raised in lone-parent households. Few would disagree that raising a child as a lone parent is harder than raising a child as a couple. In a lone-parent household, there is typically less time for one-on-one engagement with adults and less money to go around. Although friends and extended family often help out, it remains true that on many measures, children raised in lone-parent households do worse than those raised in two-parent households.[26] There are doubtless instances in which children are better off when their parents separate (such as in the case of domestic violence), but lone parents must work harder than couple families to raise their children.

Until now, I've focused on whether children are raised by one parent or two, avoiding the question of whether parents are married. Everything I have said treats de facto parents identically to married parents. Let's now turn to a thorny question about family structure: does marriage matter?

The first thing to note is that the statistics about marriage are much better. To produce the figures above about partnerships, I spent hours analysing microdata. But to find the share of children born out of wedlock, you need only look on the Australian Bureau of Statistics' website. There, you'll find that from 1971 to 2022, the share of babies born to unmarried parents rose from 9 to 40 per cent.[27] To a large extent, this is due to the decline in 'shotgun marriages'. One estimate from the 1960s suggests that one-third of first children were conceived out of wedlock, but because most couples quickly tied the knot, the share of births to unmarried parents back then was just 6 per cent.[28]

In the Indigenous community, the share is higher still. Eighty-two per cent of First Nations babies are born to unmarried parents.[29] In the Northern Territory, 92 per cent of First Nations births are to unmarried parents, and 43 per cent do not have a father's name listed on their birth certificate.[30]

Yet from a child's viewpoint, what matters is not whether his or her parents wear metal bands on their left ring fingers, but whether they are in a stable relationship. In my own circle of friends, there are half a dozen couples who were unmarried at the time of their children's birth. Three of those couples chose to get married when the children were in primary school. The other three are still unmarried. It looks to me as though the children of these relationships are doing equally well. Indeed, in an era when women increasingly keep their maiden names, I am unable to tell which parents at my children's school are married.

Yet while having parents in a stable de facto relationship is no better or worse for a child than having parents who are married, there is some evidence that de facto relationships are less stable than marriages. For example, when a US survey interviewed a random sample of unmarried parents at the time of their child's birth, a large majority intended to stay together.[31] But by the time the child turned five, only 18 per cent were married or cohabiting. In most of the other cases, either the mother or father had begun a new romantic relationship. And in 60 per cent of cases, these new relationships had led to new children. Put another way, among children whose parents were unmarried at the time of their birth, most had a new half-sibling by the time of their fifth birthday. To the extent that this pattern holds in Australia, it does suggest that the rising share of children born to unmarried parents may presage a rising share of children raised in complex or unstable households.[32]

Should all pregnancies end in marriage? Not a bit of it. My good friend Sarah found out she was pregnant a few days after breaking up with her then boyfriend.[33] Because of her firm religious views, there was no question of terminating the pregnancy. She raised her daughter on her own, then began dating again. She met another man, got married and had two more children.

It's important that the debate on family structure be grounded in high-quality evidence. In his book, former Liberal MP Kevin Andrews cites a spate of studies that purport to show that married people are more likely than unmarried people to volunteer, have better mental health, and are less likely to die of cancer.[34] I think he overstates the case, since those who marry are typically better off even *before* they tie the knot.

Another claim often made by conservatives is that the poor are having too many children (as a house guest in *The Great Gatsby* sings, 'One thing's sure and nothing's surer: the rich get richer and the poor get – children').[35] For all the times I'd seen this argument made, I had yet to observe a skerrick of evidence for it, so in the spirit of *MythBusters* I put it to the test. Using a 2022 Australian household survey, I restricted the sample to partnered women above child-bearing age (forty-five to sixty-four) and looked at how many children each woman had borne.[36] Differences exist, but they are small. For example, women in the poorest fifth of the wealth distribution had borne an average of 2.6 children, while women in the richest fifth had borne an average of 2.3. It is more common for disadvantaged women to have large families: 21 per cent of the poorest women had borne at least four children, compared with 10 per cent of the richest. But overall I found a weak relationship between family size and wealth. If all you know about a family is the number of children, chances are you will do a bad job of guessing its wealth.

Just as controversial as the issue of family structure is that of parenting style. In the United States, researchers have shown that children of higher educated parents are more likely to read books and to get a good night's sleep.[37] Affluent parents are also less likely to use corporal punishment, and more likely to be stringent about restricting screen time.[38] Observing a small sample of families with toddlers, a pair of researchers found that professional parents addressed about two thousand words per hour to their children, in contrast to the five hundred words from parents receiving welfare benefits.[39] By the age of three, the most advantaged children had heard thirty million more words from their parents than the least advantaged. The effect of this can be life-changing. As one US educator put it: 'An affluent five-year-old has about the same vocabulary as an adult living in poverty.'[40]

We know less about this issue in Australia, but the evidence seems to point in the same direction. Children from disadvantaged families are more likely to be worried about parental job loss, fighting in the family, and excessive drug and alcohol use.[41] In affluent homes, three-quarters of children report that they enjoy reading, while only half the children from disadvantaged backgrounds say the same.[42]

Parenting approach seems to drive some of these differences. Analysing Australian data, the University of Chicago researcher Ariel Kalil and her co-authors compared pre-schoolers who have university-educated mothers with those whose mothers do not have a high-school qualification.[43] They found that pre-schoolers in the first group average twenty-two minutes a day of reading and colouring, while those in the second average sixteen minutes. Six minutes a day may not sound like much, but overall it means that pre-schoolers with highly educated mothers receive nearly 40 per cent more 'teaching time'.

Kalil concluded that the difference has little to do with working hours, income or marital status. Highly educated mothers aren't parenting differently because they're richer or have more time: rather it's because of what Kalil called 'their values, knowledge, and expectations'.

The sociologist Annette Lareau describes the parenting strategy employed by highly educated parents as 'concerted cultivation'.[44] She notes that such parents are more likely to schedule activities for their children, encourage children to question adults and promote a sense of entitlement. Lower educated parents tend to employ a less pushy and more organic style of parenting, known as 'natural growth'.

Concerted cultivation can entail plenty of scheduling, as parents shuttle children between cooking classes and horse-riding lessons, violin practice and hockey training. But it also involves engaging directly with children as if they were little adults: asking them about their day and discussing with them the interactions they have had with adults. So-called helicopter parents are probably practising an intense form of concerted cultivation. Concerted cultivation is the very opposite of the old saying that 'children should be seen and not heard'. Children become the focus of the household.

Natural growth is the parenting style used to raise most Baby Boomers and almost all children born before World War II. It allows children more free time to explore their own pursuits. 'Go and play outside until dinnertime' is a sentence more likely to be associated with natural growth parenting. Less emphasis is placed on engaging with adults as equals. Kids are allowed to be kids. If you've seen the television series *Mad Men*, set in 1960s America, you'll recognise natural growth parenting. There are even movements afoot today to return to this kind of approach, such as the 'slow parenting' movement (sample book titles: *The Idle Parent: Why Less Means More When Raising Kids; Free Range Kids; Confessions of a Slacker Mom*).

Whichever of the two strategies your gut prefers, it looks like children brought up by concerted cultivation tend to do better academically and earn higher incomes as adults.[45] Moreover, as Ariel Kalil's evidence demonstrates, differences in teaching time are visible at a young age and are correlated with the educational background of the parents. These differences mean that children arrive at school with quite different levels of preparation. To me, such work screams out the need to get Australia's best teachers in front of our most disadvantaged pupils.

In her book *What Money Can't Buy*, the University of Chicago's Susan Mayer discusses how her thinking on poverty has evolved.[46] Over time, Mayer acknowledges, she came to focus less on money, and more on social and cultural explanations for poverty. My own intellectual journey on this issue has been similar. Unless we properly understand the family dynamics of poverty, I do not believe policymakers can craft effective solutions to boost social mobility.

For too long, most progressives have shied away from discussion of family structure and parenting for fear of being accused of blaming some of the hardest working people in society. But we should not ignore the body of scholarship showing that if we want to cut poverty and boost mobility, we must think seriously about what happens inside families.

So far, I've talked about the role of money, families and parenting in perpetuating social status across generations. To keep the story straightforward, I haven't discussed all the factors that affect mobility. For example, some research suggests that following your parent into the same firm is one way that social status is replicated across generations.[47] Others point to the importance of genes. While genetic factors explain around one-fifth of the transmission of income across generations, there's little likelihood that policymakers will ever tinker with your DNA.[48] Genes help determine our height, our health and our IQ, each of which has an impact on earnings.[49] But the latest wave of research suggests that gene–environment interactions have a major impact on development, indicating that we should be wary of any form of genetic determinism.[50]

And then there's education. Even at school, large achievement gaps exist between the children of lower and higher educated parents.[51] By the time they hit the labour market, the gap has grown larger still, since children with less educated parents are more likely to leave school early and less likely to complete a post-school qualification. As a friend of mine who was the first in her family to attend university once told me, it was hard for her father (a lone-parent migrant) to show her a world that he had never entered. Children such as herself 'don't even see [university] as a realistic dream. In fact, they define themselves as the kind of people that don't do those things.'[52]

For the most part, differences in educational achievement reflect money, family and parenting, but that doesn't absolve the school system from trying to redress disadvantage.[53] Finland used to ask children to choose between vocational-track and academic-track schooling at age ten. When they raised that decision point to sixteen, Finland's intergenerational mobility rose.[54] It is vital that the Australian educational system allows late-bloomers to flourish.

It would also help if private schools provided more needs-based scholarships. At present, many scholarships are based on academic performance rather than need. Non-government schools receive more government funding when they enrol a student from a disadvantaged background, but this is rarely carried over to the fees these students are charged. Another way in which independent schools perpetuate existing hierarchies is by giving preference to the sons and daughters of alumni.[55] By privileging the children of 'old boys' and 'old girls', such schools are reducing the amount of social mobility in Australia.

It's also clear that parents' views about education are transmitted to their children. Surveying teenagers and their parents, one Australian study found that when mothers thought an education was extremely important to get ahead, children were more likely to hold the same view.[56] These attitudes are likely to be one channel through which intergenerational patterns are replicated.[57] But if we are looking for 'deep' causes, then money, families and parenting will be more important.

≠

In the previous chapter, I argued for more equality – but not perfect equality. The same goes for mobility. As the economist-turned-politician Hugh Dalton pointed out in his 1925 book on inequality, families are constantly working in different ways to benefit their children.[58] Perfect equality of opportunity, Dalton argued, would require abolishing all inheritances, gifts and spending on children above a certain maximum. Indeed, he suggested that if families are helping children in important non-material ways, *perfect* equality of opportunity would require taking all children away from their parents at birth and raising them in public institutions. And yet the fact that perfect equality of opportunity is impossible and undesirable does not stop politicians of all stripes from aiming for greater equality of opportunity.

To prevent birth becoming fate, we need to think hard about money, parenting and family structure. Government policies should recognise that the way to prevent children's destinies diverging is to invest disproportionately in the neediest – in children like Isabel. But those interventions must acknowledge the powerful effects of the home environment on children's life chances.

In the conclusion, I'll discuss some specific ideas about what might help to increase mobility and reduce inequality. Before we get there, let's take a moment to look at the evidence on attitudes to inequality. How do Australians feel about the current gaps between rich and poor, and what do we think is the proper role of government?

7
What Do Australians Think About Inequality?

Let's try another version of the veil of ignorance test we did in the Introduction. Suppose you had an equal chance of being born into any of the five wealth quintiles in Australia. Would you prefer to be born into a society where the bottom fifth had 1 per cent and the top fifth had 63 per cent of the wealth? Or a society where the poor had 15 per cent and the rich had 24 per cent?

As you may recall, the first set of numbers is the actual distribution of wealth in Australia. When surveyed about their ideal distribution, though, the majority of respondents wanted the nation to be more egalitarian.[1] Indeed, the second set of figures is the preference of the *most affluent*.

In part, this is because most people believe that our wealth distribution is considerably more equal than it turns out to be. On average, Australians think that the top fifth has 40 per cent of all wealth (actually 63 per cent), while the bottom fifth has 9 per cent (actually 1 per cent). This isn't just a mistake that Australians make: a similar survey found that Americans also underestimated their level of wealth inequality.[2] Shown the wealth distributions in Sweden and the United States (without country labels), 92 per cent of US respondents preferred the former.[3]

Attitudinal surveys show a preference for greater equality, but not complete sameness. Take a survey conducted in 2019. At that time, official statistics indicate that unskilled factory workers earned around $50,000, while the chair of a large national company earned around $600,000. Asked how much people in those occupations ought to earn, the typical respondent thought the factory worker should earn $140,000 and the corporate chair should earn $879,000.[4] They wanted the pay gap between the factory floor and the corner office to be reduced.

Other surveys have asked Australians whether they agree or disagree that 'differences in income are too large'. In 2019, 73 per cent agreed, up from 66 per cent in 1994.[5] Conversely, only 13 per cent agreed that 'large differences in income are necessary for Australia's prosperity', down from 29 per cent in 1987.[6] Australians tend not to be enraged about inequality – asked how angry they feel about the wealth gap between rich and poor on a scale from one to ten, the average person gives an answer of five – but most want to see a more egalitarian nation.[7]

Increasing concern about inequality can be seen across advanced countries.[8] Moreover, those countries where inequality has risen most have seen the largest increase in the share of people who think that differences in income are too large.[9]

Another way of measuring attitudes to inequality is to show people different possible pictures of the income distribution and have them pick the one they prefer. In these exercises, only 14 per cent of respondents say that their *ideal* is a pyramid-shaped income distribution, with a few people at the top and everyone else below.[10] Yet 64 per cent of people believe that a pyramid shape *accurately describes* Australian society today.[11] We see the reality of income inequality, but the share of people who want to live in a pyramid-type society is lower than it was in the late 1980s.[12]

Perhaps one reason Australians like equal societies is that most of us think we're in the middle. A miniscule 1 per cent of people describe themselves as 'upper class', and only 8 per cent call themselves 'upper middle class'.[13] Further insight comes from a question that divided society into ten groups, and asked people which they put themselves into. Mathematically, a tenth of us must be in the top 10 per cent, but only 1 per cent placed themselves in the top group, and only 1 per cent placed themselves in the second-highest group. Over half the population say that they are in the middle 20 per cent of society.[14] Personally, our household's income puts us in the top 10 per cent. If that's your situation, I'd encourage you to be honest about it too.

We have discussed how the Rawlsian veil of ignorance would likely cause us to choose a society with relatively low levels of inequality. This is consistent with evidence from economics experiments, which show that relativities have a strong effect on people's happiness. It matches with much of what we know about the Australian psyche, which is infused with a clear preference for egalitarianism.

For many, a source of egalitarian preferences is religion. In Christianity, Luke's gospel has Jesus saying, 'Sell everything you have and give to the poor, and you will have treasure in heaven' (Luke 18:22), while Matthew's gospel says, 'It is easier for a camel to go through the eye of a needle, than for a rich man to enter into the kingdom of God' (Matthew 19:24). In his first letter to the Corinthians, Paul wrote using the Greek word *agape* – unconditional love for other humans. Paul emphasised that *agape* required kindness and tolerance, protection of the needy and unselfishness. *Agape* was, he said, greater than faith or hope (1 Corinthians 13).[15]

In a similar vein, many Muslims are guided by the injunction to share their possessions with those who have less. The Qur'an says: 'Allah has favoured some of you above others in worldly gifts. But those more favoured will not restore any part of their worldly gifts to those whom their right hands possess, so that they may be equal sharers in them. Will they then deny the favour of Allah?' (Ch.16:V.72).

Many Buddhists follow the words of the Dalai Lama: 'There can be no peace as long as there is grinding poverty, social injustice, inequality, oppression, environmental degradation, and as long as the weak and small continue to be trodden by the mighty and powerful.' Sikhism's founder, Guru Nanak, taught 'Accept all humans as your equals, and let them be your only sect' (Japji Sahib 28). Sikhism emphases the free distribution of food, a practice known as *langar*.

Religions do not preach egalitarianism in every instance, but for some people they provide an important inspiration to redress inequalities. Many of the community groups that are most passionate about providing Christmas hampers, serving breakfast to the homeless, looking after refugees and helping people with disabilities are those with a religious foundation. When COVID-19 hit, such groups provided valuable assistance to those who lacked social supports. Many of these people are also those who are most troubled by an Australia in which the affluent increasingly lose touch with the disadvantaged.

What do people believe government should do about rising inequality? Over the past quarter-century, the Australian Election Study has been asking whether we agree that 'Income and wealth should be redistributed'.[16] In 1987, the share of people who favoured redistribution was 58 per cent. As Figure 14 shows, this rose rapidly in the 1990s, peaking at 76 per cent in 2001. In 2022, 69 per cent supported redistribution.[17]

Figure 14: What should government do about inequality?

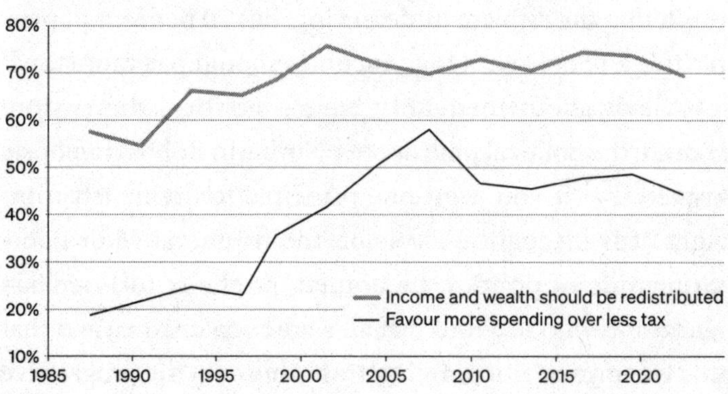

A more specific question shows a similar trend. Asked whether the government should cut taxes or spend more on social services, only 19 per cent of people in 1987 favoured additional spending.[18] But by 2007, 58 per cent preferred a spending increase to a tax cut. In 2022, 44 per cent favoured a spending boost. Given that tax cuts tend to be regressive, while social services spending tends to be progressive, one interpretation of these data is that Australians are more inclined to curb inequality than they were in the 1980s.

Other surveys point in the same direction. Asked in 2019 whether 'It is the responsibility of the government to reduce the differences in income between people with high incomes and those with low incomes,' 57 per cent agreed – a slightly higher share than had been recorded a decade earlier.[19] Similar views apply to corporations, with 63 per cent agreeing that 'it is the responsibility of private companies to reduce the differences in pay between their employees with high pay and those with low pay'.[20] Australians don't tend to think that the rich are undeserving, but 70 per cent of people think people with high incomes should pay more tax.[21]

Views about inequality have a political dimension. Indeed, the political philosopher Norberto Bobbio famously argued that if you want one principle to divide left from right, it is inequality. Those on the conservative or libertarian side of politics, he argued, are heirs to Friedrich Nietzsche, who believed that all were born unequal and that this was a good thing. By contrast, those on the progressive or social-democratic side are heirs to Jean-Jacques Rousseau, who believed that all were born equal and that many of the inequalities we observe come from social institutions. In other words, the right condemns social equality because of a belief in natural inequality, while the left condemns social inequality because of a belief in natural equality.[22]

In saying this, Bobbio isn't arguing that people on the right of politics will always defend inequality, or that people on the left will always strive for perfect equality. In Australia, his point simply translates into saying that your attitudes to inequality are a pretty good predictor of whether you'll vote for Labor or the Coalition.[23]

Recent statistical evidence supports this point. In a survey conducted after the 2022 election, 64 per cent of Labor voters said they believe that income and wealth should be redistributed, in contrast to 36 per cent of Coalition voters.[24] The difference is even greater among politicians. An anonymous survey of federal parliamentary candidates conducted in 2019 found that 83 per cent of Labor candidates agreed that income and wealth should be redistributed, compared with 7 per cent of Coalition candidates.[25]

Anecdotal evidence backs this up. Labor prime minister Anthony Albanese has argued that 'We need to ensure that as our nation's wealth grows, the benefits are shared more equally', while his treasurer, Jim Chalmers, has noted that 'without dedicated action, inequality in one generation breeds inequality in the next'.[26] Former Labor treasurer Wayne Swan has argued that reducing inequality is the 'central and abiding purpose of the Labor cause today', pointing out that equity is a consistent theme in the music of Bruce Springsteen, Cold Chisel and the Hilltop Hoods.[27]

By contrast, former Liberal prime ministers have been more sanguine about inequality. John Howard once commented that 'It's very important to get this income distribution thing in perspective. To the extent that any gaps have widened, it has been that people at the top – there are more of them, and they're doing better.'[28] Tony Abbott took the view that 'in the end we have to be a productive and competitive society and greater inequality might be inevitable.'[29] Robert Menzies famously distinguished between 'leaners' and 'lifters', a theme taken up by Liberal treasurer Joe Hockey when delivering the 2014 budget, perhaps the most regressive budget in living memory.[30]

Political debates about inequality in Australia display both a partisan pattern and a secular trend. To see this more precisely, I searched the federal parliamentary debates and recorded the number of times the word 'inequality' has been mentioned in either the House of Representatives or the Senate since Federation. The word has appeared over five thousand times (although not all these mentions relate to economic inequality).[31] To make a comparison over time, I adjusted according to the amount of time parliament sat each year.[32] The parliamentary mentions are charted in Figure 15, averaged to a hundred. Years in which a federal Labor government was in office for most of the year are marked with bars.

The frequency of inequality debates declined during the first two decades after Federation (perhaps because the focus was on establishing Commonwealth institutions,

Figure 15: Parliamentary mentions of inequality

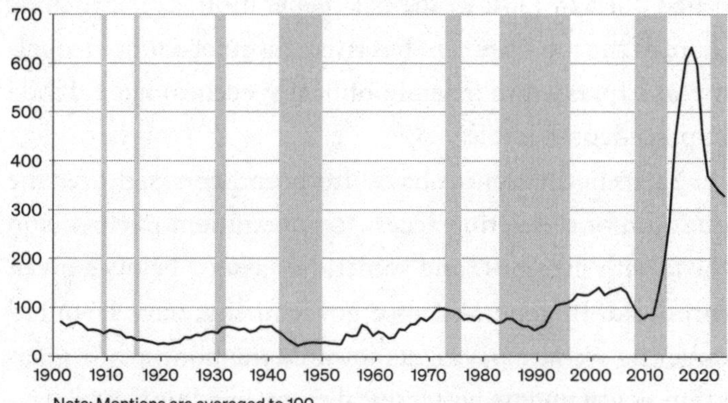

Note: Mentions are averaged to 100.
Shaded bars denote years in which Labor was in office for a majority of the year.

and then dealing with World War I). Inequality was often talked about during the Great Depression of the 1930s, but then little debated in the post-war decades. From the 1970s onwards, inequality has been mentioned more often in parliament, although there was a modest decline in the late 1980s, followed by a sharp rise that coincided with the early 1990s recession. In the past half century, the discussion of inequality appears to be more common under conservative governments. Parliamentary mentions of inequality rose under the Coalition government of John Howard (1996–2007) and soared during the Coalition governments of Tony Abbott, Malcolm Turnbull and Scott Morrison (2013–22). At its peak in 2018, inequality was mentioned six times more frequently than the average since Federation.

These trends are not specific to politicians; they also reflect shifts in the national mood.[33] It was not until the

1970s that concern about inequality returned to the level it had been in 1901. In the past generation, as the income share of the top 1 per cent has risen, disquiet about inequality (as expressed in federal political speeches) has reached unprecedented levels.

Partisan differences have also been expressed over the question of restricting access to government payments to those with incomes (and sometimes assets) below a given threshold. In general, Labor governments have favoured targeting welfare payments towards the poor, while Coalition governments have typically preferred universal payments.[34] While targeted welfare is generally regarded by economists as being more equitable and more efficient, it involves denying some voters payments. Episodes of means-testing have therefore seen governments criticised heavily by their opponents.

For example, when Bob Hawke's Labor government sought to reintroduce the pension assets test in the 1980s, the Opposition leader Andrew Peacock described assets-testing as a 'callous and cynical grab for funds' that was one of 'the assaults the Government has made on the elderly'.[35] The Coalition's shadow minister for social security said that an assets test was 'penalising thrift'.[36]

Under John Howard's Coalition government, the trend was in the opposite direction. Near-universal family payments were expanded. Universal payments such as the First Homeowner Grant, the Baby Bonus and the Private Health Insurance Rebate were introduced. Similarly, under Scott Morrison's Coalition government, the largest pandemic support measure was JobKeeper, a flat-rate payment. Only one-quarter of JobKeeper payments ended up in the pockets of workers, with the remaining three-quarters supporting the profits of businesses, some of which used it to pay executive bonuses.[37]

Means-testing by the Rudd and Gillard Labor governments was met with criticism from the Coalition. When the government means-tested the Baby Bonus to exclude the top 6 per cent of families, Malcolm Turnbull called it 'an appeal to Labor's divisive envy politics'.[38] After Labor froze indexation on a Family Tax Benefit supplement and scaled back the Dependent Spouse Tax Offset, Joe Hockey said 'I despise this envy; this envy and this jealousy.'[39] When the Baby Bonus was scaled back for second and subsequent children, a Coalition frontbencher called the decision 'vicious and savage', while Hockey compared it to China's former One Child Policy.[40] The practical politics of reducing inequality are not straightforward.

In 1901, visiting Frenchman Albert Métin was struck by the debate over inequality in Australia. European reformers, he noted, were happy to call themselves socialists and to discuss philosophy. But when theoretical arguments were put to Australian progressives, he said, they 'ignore or run away from them'. When Métin asked one worker to sum up his program, the man replied, 'My program! *Ten bob a day!*'[41]

This practical egalitarianism marks many aspects of Australian life. On virtually every war memorial erected in the past century, soldiers are listed alphabetically. Typically, rank isn't mentioned.[42] Everyone who serves Australia in battle earns the title 'digger'. In World War I, Australians' refusal to salute British officers when off-duty caused frequent confrontations. A British officer observed that he had never met troops so unimpressed by senior rank.[43] Another mark of our egalitarianism is the fact that Australian soldiers went on strike during World War I, action that would have been unthinkable in more hierarchical nations.[44]

As we saw in earlier chapters, Australia experienced high levels of inequality at the time of World War I. Yet in the 1950 and 1960s, some accounts implied that inequality had become an irrelevancy.[45] But by the 1990s, the gap between rich and poor was back on the public radar. As one study participant put it:

> class distinctions are creeping back into Australian society. Although we like to think of Australia as being an egalitarian society, it is surprising how often you hear people saying things which suggest that they really think they are in a different class from the rest of us.[46]

In recent decades, Australia's preoccupation with the ways of the rich is apparent just from our viewing habits. Popular television programs include *Top Gear* (promoting expensive cars), *The Block* and *Selling Houses Australia* (in which people renovate soon-to-be expensive houses) and *Dancing with the Stars* (showcasing affluent celebrities).

My review of public opinion data demonstrates that a majority of Australians believe that differences in income are too large. Respondents would prefer a more equal distribution of earnings, and even the affluent would prefer a less skewed wealth distribution. Most people think that government and private companies have an obligation to reduce inequality, and seven out of ten of us say that income and wealth should be redistributed to ordinary working people. These concerns stem from both religious and secular values, and have been reflected in the political realm, where inequality is being debated more than ever. Yet as the politics of means-testing illustrates, policies to reduce inequality are often controversial. It is to these solutions that I finally turn.

8. What Is to Be Done?

In 2002, two bombs exploded in Bali nightclubs, killing and injuring hundreds of people. At the local hospital, there was a shortage of painkillers. Graeme Southwick, an Australian doctor on duty, asked patients to assess their own pain levels. He kept being told by patients in the 'Australian' ward that they were okay – the person next to them was suffering more.

Coming across this account, the historian John Hirst was reminded of the description of injured Australians in Gallipoli nearly a century earlier.[1] He quotes the official war historian Charles Bean, who describes the suffering and then says, 'Yet the men never showed better than in these difficulties. The lightly hurt were full of thought for the severely wounded.' Even in the midst of their own pain, the first instinct of many Australians was to think of those worse off than themselves.

A sceptic might suggest that Bean viewed our men's suffering through patriotic glasses, or that the wounded soldiers of other nations behaved similarly. But Australia's egalitarian spirit shows up in other places too. A successful Australian entrepreneur once claimed that the competitive nature of sport proved Australians didn't believe in reducing inequality, arguing that 'We do not handicap an athlete because they are abnormally fast'.[2] But it turns out that this is exactly how our sports often operate. Many Australian team sports have salary caps, while many individual sports have handicap systems. As any golfer can tell you, handicaps make the game more fun, because they allow people of different abilities to compete with one another.

We don't just handicap people. Australia's favourite horse race, the Melbourne Cup, literally puts lead in the saddlebags. Horses must carry at least forty-nine kilograms, and extra weight is put on horses that have already performed well. Racing historians celebrate Carbine, who won the 1890 Cup with a whopping sixty-six kilograms of lead in his saddlebags. By contrast, America's most famous race, the Kentucky Derby, does not add weight based on a horse's past performance.[3] The Melbourne Cup is a more egalitarian race than the Kentucky Derby.

As I noted in Chapter 2, Australian beliefs about inequality even explain why Rugby League split from Rugby Union in the early twentieth century. Because Union refused to allow player payments, it was a fine game for private schoolboys, but no way for a working-class man to make a living. For the remainder of the twentieth century, League dominated Union in the key states of New South Wales and Queensland. In the United Kingdom, a similar split occurred, but League never became as dominant.

In the 1850s, an English gold-digger wrote home that 'Rank and title have no charms in the Antipodes.'[4] In the 1880s, an essayist opined that Australia

> is the true republic – the truest, as I take it, in the world ... In England the average man feels that he is an inferior, in America that he is a superior; in Australia he feels that he is an equal. That is indeed delightful.[5]

The father of the Australian novel, Joseph Furphy, wrote in 1903 that human equality was 'self-evident ... and impregnable as any mathematical axiom.'[6] Legend had it that Australia was the nation where Jack was as good as his master – if not better.

Egalitarianism has characterised the Australian national identity for well over 150 years – dating back to an era when the country was quite unequal. Similar sentiments were being expressed in other settler societies, such as Canada and the United States, but Australia's powerful labour movement did more to make them a reality. After becoming more unequal in the late nineteenth and early twentieth centuries, Australia reached a turning point. From the 1920s to the 1970s, we steadily became a more equal society. But since then, Australia has become more unequal, with the income share of the top 1 per cent doubling and that of the top 0.1 per cent tripling.

Part of the purpose of this book is to stir a debate about inequality. One of my greatest fears is that we will sleepwalk into a more unequal Australia without realising what is being lost. As the social researcher Hugh Mackay put it in the late 1990s:

> There is now a widespread belief … that both rich and poor Australians are becoming more numerous and that if the gap between them grows much wider, it may well turn out to be unbridgeable. Such a prospect is so disturbing to the Australian people – and so incompatible with their dreams – that they are reluctant to discuss it.[7]

We need to be careful that we do not unwittingly lose something that past generations of Australians have held sacred.

So how should we go about reducing inequality? First, we must maintain the policy expertise that has delivered solid economic growth over recent decades. Without improved productivity, we cannot continue to increase average incomes per person. Sluggish economies often hurt the most disadvantaged, with the unskilled most likely to be jobless, and the poor most at risk when social services are pared back. Australia's economic growth has been based on more than good luck. It has relied on a commitment to open markets – welcoming foreign investment, migrants and imported products. And it has depended on policies that encourage innovation, which means good public infrastructure, along with appropriate regulations and incentives to carry out research and development.

Second, we must improve our education system. As a society, we need to recognise that there's nothing equal about a race in which people start from different points. Equality of opportunity doesn't mean making the strongest competitors run in gumboots, but it might mean buying a pair of runners for someone who can't afford them.[8] As technology advances, our education system has to do more – particularly for the most disadvantaged. Early intervention programs and a better education system are vital to reducing inequality.

As I discussed in Chapter 4, although educational attainment has risen, large gaps remain between children from rich and poor backgrounds. By the time children reach Year 9, the attainment gap between those with parents in high-status occupations and those whose parents are jobless equates to three to four years.[9] The attainment gap between children with higher and lower educated parents is similarly large. We know that a child from a poor background has a lower chance of finishing high school, but these figures suggest that even if they do complete their schooling, there will be a massive gap in their understanding of the curriculum.[10] The typical Year 12 student from a disadvantaged background will read at the same level as the typical Year 8 student from an advantaged background, and their maths ability will match the average Year 9 student from a well-off family.

This stands as a brutally high barrier to further study for many disadvantaged pupils. With lower test scores, it is more difficult to win a place at university, and more difficult for those who do enrol to graduate. From 2008 to 2022, the achievement gap in grade-three reading between advantaged and disadvantaged students widened by almost a full year of achievement.[11] It is vital that we improve educational opportunities for children from poor backgrounds. These might include incentives for the best teachers to work in the most disadvantaged schools, better programs to keep young people engaged, and high-quality early childhood programs for extremely disadvantaged children.

Third, we need to acknowledge the role that family structure plays in perpetuating advantage and disadvantage across generations. But we need to be sure that solutions don't just compound the problems, because raising children as a lone parent is tough enough without adding to the social stigma. We should build up the evidence on light-touch programs that encourage relationship stability, rather than making it harder to get a divorce. Similarly, the evidence on parenting investments shouldn't be taken as a licence to intervene in complex household decisions, but as a pointer towards trialling ways of encouraging a little more 'concerted cultivation' in the most disadvantaged households.

Fourth, it's worth recognising the role that unions play in reducing inequality. Throughout their history, unions have advocated most strongly for the lowest paid workers. That has traditionally meant arguing not only for greater pay equality, but also for more equity in conditions. In past generations, unions have argued that workers at the bottom of the income scale deserved the right to time off when they were sick, an annual holiday and superannuation so they could enjoy a decent retirement – all conditions that had long been enjoyed by higher paid employees. Recent years have seen unions fighting for pay equity across sectors – successfully arguing, for example, that workers in the female-dominated social and community sector were being underpaid relative to male-dominated occupations.

A healthy union movement does not require going back to 'closed shops', in which employees could not get a job without first joining the union. Such arrangements not only violated the principle of free association; they also encouraged laziness on the part of management and union leaders. Today's union movement recognises that it needs to work hard to attract and keep members, and the best union leaders are experimenting with new ways to boost membership. Unions also rely on laws that give them the chance to persuade new employees to sign up, which means the ability to enter workplaces, play a role in wage negotiations and conduct safety inspections.[12]

Fifth, we need to make sure that welfare spending continues to be targeted towards those most in need. Since the start of the millennium, one of the few countries that has reduced inequality is Brazil. Although inequality is still high there, it's going in the opposite direction to that of many other countries. One reason for this, according to the experts, is that Brazil did a better job of targeting its welfare spending towards the poor.[13]

In Australia, a tradition of means-tested social payments has meant that our welfare system is more progressive than that of any other advanced nation.[14] The average advanced country gives twice as much welfare to the bottom fifth of the population as to the top fifth, while Australia gives twelve times as much to the poor as to the rich.

Yet as the discussion in Chapter 7 illustrates, the politics of means-testing will continue to be difficult.[15] Standard political theories suggest that elections are won by focusing on 'the median voter', not by targeting the most disadvantaged. There will always be pressure on governments to relax means-testing and expand universal rather than targeted programs. But when governments focus on the neediest, it's possible to reduce the gap between the poor and the middle. For example, the Rudd government's decision in 2009 to boost the single age pension (which is means-tested and assets-tested) by over $1600 a year reduced by one-fifth the share of people in poverty.[16]

Sixth, we need to maintain a progressive income tax system, in which those who earn more pay a higher tax rate than those with lower incomes. Progressive taxes recognise that those on higher incomes have more discretionary income. High incomes may be a reflection of effort, but they are also sometimes a product of good fortune, which is why one economist has proposed that we index our tax scales to inequality.[17] Moreover, the further up the income scale you are, the more capacity you have to fund our schools, military, hospitals and pensions. And while higher income people are lighter users of the income support system, they tend to be heavier users of other public services, including universities, roads and airports.

According to one study, the inequality-reducing effect of the Australian tax system fell slightly between 2001 and 2016.[18] As economists point out, it makes more sense to carry out redistribution through the income tax system than through other taxes.[19] Tempting as it is to achieve redistribution via environmental, consumption or company taxes, this ends up being extremely inefficient. We can achieve outcomes that are more equitable – and more efficient – if we maintain a strongly progressive income tax system. Flattening the income tax scales will increase demands to use less efficient taxes to achieve the same goals.

Seventh, the way to improve social policies is to evaluate them well. At present, too many evaluations are low quality, such as naive before–after studies.[20] Testing new social policies by means of medical-style randomised trials would provide better information about what works. Randomised trials are compulsory for pharmaceuticals, but almost non-existent for social policies (although a new Australian Centre for Evaluation is trying to change that).

Raising the evidence bar isn't just about a better feedback loop; it also embodies a more modest approach to politics. If we knew everything about how to help the truly disadvantaged, we wouldn't have multi-generational poverty cycles, wide educational achievement gaps and a growing jail population. If we believe Australia should be more equal, then we need to combine optimism about addressing the problem with realism about the ability of any particular policy to get there.

Eighth, we need to keep a check on monopoly power. Monopolies overcharge customers and underpay suppliers. Too often, they focus on building anti-competitive 'moats' to keep out new entrants. The poorest consumers can suffer the most. If you're on a tight budget, it's tough to buy in bulk or find the cheapest stores. Peddling false hope among the vulnerable, some scams deliberately target poor communities.

Strong competition laws aren't just vital for consumers; they're important for workers too. Monopsony power arises when employees have only a few job choices – allowing firms to pay people less than they're worth. One in five Australian workers is subject to a non-compete clause that hampers their ability to move to a better job (and a bigger pay packet). A more competitive economy is good for both productivity and equality.

Ninth, it is vital to recognise the link between inequality and social isolation. As Nick Terrell and I documented in *Reconnected: A Community Builder's Handbook*, Australia has suffered a drop in civic connectedness over the past generation. People are less likely to play an organised sport, less likely to attend a religious service and less likely to volunteer. The typical Australian today has only about half as many close friends as in the mid-1980s.

Equality and community are two sides of the same coin. One survey asked Australians how often they met people a lot richer or a lot poorer than themselves. Almost half said that in the typical week, they did not encounter people who were a lot richer or a lot poorer.[21] When we live more isolated lives, it's harder to close the income gap. A more connected society is likely to be a more equal one too.

Tenth, we need to keep egalitarianism at the heart of our national story. A belief in equality has been a golden thread through Australia's history, even at times when the gap between rich and poor has widened. It is vital that egalitarianism stay at the core of our country's ethos.

National identity is shaped by stories. Some are symbolic nuggets. Peter FitzSimons recounts the tale of a conversation with Bob Hawke, in which an insistent waitress twice interrupted the then prime minister in mid-sentence to take his coffee order. Only in Australia, FitzSimons thought to himself.

Our big national episodes matter too. The 1854 Eureka Rebellion – a collective uprising against oppressive taxation – should be reclaimed by both sides of politics as our driving legend.[22] It recognises that hard-working entrepreneurs are vital to our nation's success. And it tells of the willingness of protestors to join with their mates in a cause greater than themselves: a fairer Australia. With a strong egalitarian spirit, there is more chance that Australia will reduce economic inequality.

≠

Inequality may loom larger than any of us, but creating a fairer society is something that happens on a very human scale. Something as simple as a great teacher in a disadvantaged school can change a life forever. Here's what one Melbourne girl wrote to her English teacher:

> you were the only teacher that believed in me ... I was doubted, labelled dumb/stupid and put down constantly in every class, except in Writer's Workshop. You created an environment that made each student special,

> like they belonged in the class ... I know I never spoke about personal things but you and Writer's Workshop changed my life just before I had given up. Things at home have even gotten better since I joined your class ... Never forget that by treating young adults/teenagers like equals or as a friend and just simply believing in them you'll give them faith, hope, dreams and inspiration.[23]

Ultimately, the choice for Australia is summed up by the differences between two football leagues. Do we want a society that looks like the English Premier League, with a winner-takes-all approach and the same teams taking out the championship most years? Or do we want to emulate the Australian Football League, with rules that reduce inequality, increase competitive balance and make the game more interesting?

The past generation has seen many successes for the Australian economy. We are more productive and entrepreneurial, more open to ideas, products and people from overseas. But at the same time, we have become more unequal. There are many things about the 1950s and 1960s that we would not want to keep, but it's worth trying to reclaim those high levels of equality. Too much inequality strains the social fabric, threatening to cleave us one from another. Australia is a stronger nation when we act together than when we pull apart.

Acknowledgements

My interest in inequality and social policy was piqued by Harvard's Christopher ('Sandy') Jencks, whose sparkling prose persuaded me that the topic was both worthy and fascinating. Sandy became my PhD thesis supervisor, and was instrumental in encouraging my collaboration with Oxford's Sir Tony Atkinson, with whom I worked on several projects analysing top incomes, before sadly passing away in 2017. By coincidence, both Sandy and Tony published seminal books on inequality in 1972, the year of my birth.[1] At Harvard, I participated in a multidisciplinary seminar on inequality (the sociologists had the best questions, the economists the best answers, and the political scientists told us why it would never get through Congress). David Ellwood, Caroline Hoxby, Jeff Liebman, Larry Katz, Jeff Williamson and Robert Putnam taught me much about why inequality matters, and how to analyse the issues you'll read about in this book.

When I graduated with my PhD, it was Deborah Cobb-Clark who coaxed me to the Australian National University, where I found a group of colleagues who challenged my ideas and methods at every turn. I loved it. Thanks in particular to Alison Booth, Bob Breunig, Bruce Chapman,

Paul Frijters, Bob Gregory, Tim Hatton, Warwick McKibbin and Chris Ryan for making me a better researcher. Supported by Australian Research Council grants, I was fortunate enough to have three full-time research assistants working with me: Elena Varganova, Susanne Schmidt and Jenny Chesters.

As a parliamentarian, I have appreciated the research skills of the Parliamentary Library and have been ably assisted by a group of whip-smart young people who worked with me, including Jack Brady, Daniel Carr, Tanya Greeves, Michael Jones, Ben Molan and Jacob White. I'm also grateful to Deanna Cronk and her team at the National Library of Australia's document delivery service for copying reams of pages from past *BRW* magazines, and Lisa Fittock and Sue Satsia in the Australian Taxation Office library for helping me get tabulations of inheritance-tax returns going back to the 1950s.

As a user of the Household, Income and Labour Dynamics in Australia survey, I am required to acknowledge that this book uses unit record data from that survey, which was initiated and is funded by the Australian Government Department of Social Services and is managed by the Melbourne Institute of Applied Economic and Social Research. The findings and views reported in this book, however, are those of the author and should not be attributed to the Australian government, Department of Social Services or the Melbourne Institute. Ann Evans supplied me with unpublished tabulations from the 2009 and 2011 Australian Surveys of Social Attitudes, Ian McAllister provided me with analysis from the 2019 Australian Candidate Study and Nigel Stapledon kindly updated his long-run house-price series. Special mentions go to my anonymous parliamentary colleague and my anonymous friend for sharing the personal stories that appear in Chapter 6, and to Jacinta Mudge for allowing me to quote her letter to her teacher, Liam Wood. Speaking of sharing, researchers who would like to use any data from this book are encouraged to contact me.

I've learned a great deal, too, from my inequality co-authors. As well as Atkinson and Jencks, I've relished inequality collaborations with Dan Andrews, Philip Clarke, Joshua Gans, Cathy Gong, Lachlan Hotchin, Pamela Katic, Xin Meng, Alberto Posso, Mike Pottenger, Martin Schmalz, Tim Smeeding, Adam Triggs, Pierre Van Der Eng and Roger Wilkins.

One of the manifestations of Australia's egalitarian spirit is the strong interest in inequality among academics. Beyond my co-authors, I've enjoyed the chance to discuss inequality and Australian economic history with Fred Argy, Rob Bray, Geoffrey Blainey, Nick Carney, Matt Cowgill, John Dickson, Diane Hutchinson, John Hirst, Kirrily Jordan, Paul Kauffman, William Rubinstein, UNSW's Peter Saunders, Michael Schneider, Frank Stilwell, Mark Thomas, Avi Waksberg, Peter Whiteford and Glenn Withers. I have learned a great deal from my Labor colleagues, for whom egalitarianism is a defining mission.

My editor Chris Feik is a wholly wise and wonderful wordsmith. My thanks to him and the team at Black Inc., including Duncan Blachford, Marilyn de Castro, Kate Hatch, Nikola Lusk, Kate Nash, Denise O'Dea and Elisabeth Young. A suite of savvy reviewers also provided thoughtful feedback. Thanks particularly to Dan Andrews, Jeff Borland, Rob Bray, Claire Daly, Lin Hatfield Dodds, Macgregor Duncan, Joshua Gans, Murray Goot, Tanya Greeves, Tim Hatton, John Hirst, Jessica Irvine, Christopher Jencks, Christopher Joye, Ian Keen, Barbara Leigh, Michael Leigh, Gus Little, Jane Mansbridge, Ben Molan, William Rubinstein, Peter Saunders, Colin Soskolne, Frank Stilwell, Nick Terrell, Roger Wilkins and Jeff Williamson. They won't all agree with what's written here, but I truly appreciate the time they took to read over chapter drafts. In revising *Battlers and Billionaires*, I especially benefited from the insights of Jeff Borland, Michael Coelli, Saul Eslake, Murray Goot, Tim Hatton, Laura Panza, Peter Siminski and Roger Wilkins.

As you'll see in the conclusion, I believe that one way to address inequality is to subject more social policies to randomised trials. To show how useful randomised trials can be, I chose between two possible titles for this book by running Google ads for each of them, and selecting the title with the higher click-through rate. Thanks to Barbara Leigh for suggesting *Battlers and Billionaires* in the first place.

Finally, my enduring appreciation to my wife Gweneth for our egalitarian partnership, and to our sons, Sebastian, Theodore and Zachary, for reminding me every day that relativities really do matter.

Notes

Introduction

1 Gavan Daws, cited in John Hirst, 2010, *The Australians: Insiders and Outsiders on the National Character Since 1770*, second edition, Black Inc., Melbourne, pp. 144–45.
2 Tom Uren, *House of Representatives Hansard*, 26 February 1959.
3 Peter Kieseker, 1993, *Peacekeeping: Challenges for the Future*, cited in Hirst, *The Australians* (see note 1, Introduction), pp. 57–58.
4 Some of these examples draw upon Craig McGregor, quoted in Hirst, *The Australians*, pp. 165–66.
5 The taxi example has a long lineage: see R.W. Connell, 1974, 'Images of Australia', in Donald E. Edgar (ed.), *Social Change in Australia*, Cheshire, Melbourne.
6 Tim Flannery, 1994, *The Future Eaters*, quoted in Hirst, *The Australians* (see note 1, Introduction), p. 191.
7 The relative rarity of the word 'sir' in Australia has been noted by other observers in 1903 and 1970: see Sol Encel, 1970, *Equality and Authority: A Study of Class, Status and Power in Australia*, Tavistock, London, p. 83 (who cites P.F. Rowland's account of Australia in 1903).
8 Frank Bongiorno, 2012, 'What We Talk about When We Talk about Bogans', *The Canberra Times*, 27 March 2012, p. 15–18.
9 Alexis de Tocqueville, 1835 [2007], *Democracy in America*, translated by Henry Reeve, Digireads, Stilwell, KS, p. 390. I am grateful to Daniel Carr for reminding me of this quote.
10 Jan Pen, 1973, 'A parade of dwarfs (and a few giants)' in A.B. Atkinson, ed., *Wealth, Income and Inequality: Selected Readings*, Penguin Books, Middlesex, pp. 73–82. Wealth distribution data from ABS, 2022, *Household Income and Wealth, Australia: Summary of Results, 2019–20*, ABS, Canberra. Wealth is scaled up by a factor of 1.414, to account for the increase in average household wealth from 2019–20 to December 2024 (I use ABS estimates of average household worth up to June 2023, and extrapolate for a further eighteen months). Average height is 1.68 metres, from ABS, 2022, *National Health Survey, 2022*, ABS, Canberra.
11 The Fitzgerald quote appeared in his 1925 short story 'Rich Boy'. Hemingway's mocking rejoinder was in his 1936 short story 'The Snows of Kilimanjaro'. Accounts of the exchange taking place in person are apocryphal.

12 The *BRW* rich list also included the Murdoch family as passing the $1 billion mark in 1987. The *BRW* rich list continued to include Rupert Murdoch and his family until 1995, despite the fact that Murdoch renounced his Australian citizenship in 1985.
13 1960s estimate based on the 1966–68 Australian Survey of Consumer Finances and Expenditures, reported in Nripesh Podder and Nanak Kakwani, 1976, 'Distribution of Wealth in Australia', *Review of Income and Wealth*, Vol. 22, No. 1, pp. 75–92, Table 14. Contemporary estimate based on ABS, 2022, *Household Income and Wealth, Australia*, 2019–20, ABS, Canberra.
14 Facundo Alvaredo, Lucas Chancel, Thomas Piketty, Emmanuel Saez and Gabriel Zucman, 2018, *World Inequality Report 2018*, Harvard University Press, Cambridge, MA, p. 241.
15 Nicholas Kristof, 2012, 'A Failed Experiment', *The New York Times*, 21 November.
16 Rich Benjamin, 2012, 'The Gated Community Mentality', *The New York Times*, 30 March 2012, p. A27; Hannah Frishberg, 2024, 'Inside the hyper-exclusive Florida enclave only the richest billionaires — like Jeff Bezos and Ivanka Trump — can call home', *New York Post*, 4 January 2024.
17 To obtain this estimate, I take the ABS's most recent figures for gross household income, which are $792 per week at the twentieth percentile and $1786 at the median in 2019–20 (ABS, 2022, *Household Income and Wealth, Australia, 2019–20*, ABS, Canberra). Income is scaled up by a factor of 1.204, to account for the increase in average household income from 2019–20 to December 2024 (I use ABS estimates of average household income up to June 2023, and extrapolate for a further eighteen months).
18 Average total individual income was $275,555 in postcode 2028 (which includes Double Bay), $234,087 in postcode 3142 (which includes Toorak), and $312,128 in postcode 6011 (which includes Cottesloe). This compares with $41,877 in postcode 2403 (which includes Myall Creek), $44,237 in postcode 5113 (which includes Elizabeth Park) and $45,611 in postcode 3047 (which includes Broadmeadows): Australian Taxation Statistics, 2023, *Individuals Statistics*, Table 25.
19 Andrew Burrell, 2012, 'Gina Rinehart Tells Whingers: Get out of the Pub', *The Australian*, 30 August.
20 Gina Rinehart, 2012, *Northern Australia and Then Some: Changes We Need to Make Our Country Rich*, Institute of Public Affairs, Melbourne.
21 For an interesting discussion of both Hancock and Rinehart, see William Finnegan, 2013, 'The Miner's Daughter', *The New Yorker*, 25 March 2013.
22 *BRW* rich list, *Business Review Weekly* magazine, 17 May 1991, p. 149.
23 The quote (and a persuasive rebuttal) is in Bernard Lagan, 2012, 'Holes in the Fabric of the Hancock Legend', *The Global Mail*, 3 September 2012.
24 Those with household incomes from $12,000 to $20,000 have on average ten missing teeth, while those in households with incomes over $80,000 have on average three missing teeth. See Australian Institute of Health and Welfare, 2011, *Oral Health and Dental Care in Australia, Key Facts and*

Figures 2011, AIHW, Canberra, p. 7 (more recent updates of the publication have not provided information on missing teeth by income).

25 Alan Duncan, 2022, 'Behind the Line: Poverty and disadvantage in Australia 2022', Bankwest Curtin Economics Centre Focus on the States Series, Report 9, Curtin University, Perth.

26 Philip Clarke and Andrew Leigh, 2011, 'Death, Dollars and Degrees: Socio-economic Status and Longevity in Australia', *Economic Papers*, Vol. 30, No. 3, pp. 348–355. Ours is the first Australian study to track individual mortality, using deaths of respondents in the longitudinal Household, Income and Labour Dynamics in Australia (HILDA) survey, which then allows us to return to earlier survey waves and compare the incomes of those who died with those who did not.

27 There are a range of possible explanations for this gap, including differences in behaviours (for example, exercise or smoking), quality of diet and access to health care and medicines. Most intriguing is a series of studies that suggest that the stress of poverty may shorten telomeres (molecular caps on chromosomes), thereby reducing a person's life. See, for example, Paul G. Shiels et al., 2011, 'Accelerated Telomere Attrition Is Associated with Relative Household Income, Diet and Inflammation in the pSoBid Cohort', *PloS ONE* 6(7), e22521.

28 The questions categorised 'Political Engagement' are from the 2022 Australian Election Study (AES). All activity questions relate to the previous five years. The question about interest in the election campaign sums those who say that they had 'a good deal' or 'some' interest. Political knowledge is based on six true or false questions (with skipped questions counted as wrong). Income in the AES is gross family income, so the three groups are up to $60,000, $60,001–$120,000 and above $120,000. All AES analysis is weighted to the 18+ citizen population. The remaining questions are from the 2022 HILDA survey, with groups split based on household disposable income, and all analyses using household weights.

29 The experiment on poverty and borrowing worked as follows. Researchers randomly split participants into two groups, and asked them to play a slingshot computer game (akin to Angry Birds). The 'rich' group members were allowed fifteen shots – the 'poor' group just three shots. The researchers then gave participants a chance to take an extra shot in the current round by giving up two shots later (essentially borrowing at a 100 per cent interest rate). The poor group were twelve times as likely to borrow as the rich, and ended up with lower scores as a result. Anuj Shah, Sendhil Mullainathan and Eldar Shafir, 2012, 'Some Consequences of Having Too Little', *Science*, Vol. 338, No. 6107, pp. 682–85. I am grateful to John Dickson for drawing this study to my attention.

30 Australian Bureau of Statistics, 2023, 'Personal Income in Australia: Regional data on the number of income earners, amounts received, and the distribution of income, 2020–21 financial year', ABS, Canberra, 6 December, Table 2.1 (all comparisons based on Gini coefficients).

31 Australian Bureau of Statistics, 'Personal Income in Australia' (note 30), Table 2.5 (all comparisons based on Gini coefficients).

32 Branko Milanovic, 2012, 'Global Income Inequality by the Numbers: In History and Now', Policy Research Working Paper 6259, World Bank, Washington DC. See also David Dollar and Aart Kraay, 2002, 'Spreading the Wealth', *Foreign Affairs*, Vol. 81, pp. 120–33.

33 Lucas Chancel, Thomas Piketty, Emmanuel Saez and Gabriel Zucman, 2022, *World Inequality Report 2022*, Harvard University Press, Cambridge, MA, p.10, Milanovic, 'Global Income Inequality by the Numbers' (see note 32, Introduction). Analysing wealth produces a similar result. The top 1 per cent own 40 per cent of world wealth: James B. Davies, Susanna Sandström, Anthony Shorrocks and Edward N. Wolff, 2008, 'The World Distribution of Household Wealth', in James B. Davies (ed.), *Personal Wealth from a Global Perspective*, Oxford University Press, New York, pp. 395–418. Australians make up 4 per cent of the world's wealthiest 1 per cent, despite constituting only 0.4 per cent of the world's population: Giles Keating, Michael O'Sullivan, Anthony Shorrocks, James Davies, Rodrigo Lluberas and Antonios Koutsoukis, 2011, *Global Wealth Report 2011*, Credit Suisse Research Institute, Zurich, p. 49.

Chapter 1

1 Quoted in Richard Broome, 1994, *Aboriginal Australians: A History Since 1788*, second edition., Allen and Unwin, St Leonards, NSW, pp. 9–21.

2 Translating Indigenous living standards into today's terms, one study puts average incomes before 1788 at $1.80 per person per day, not much more than the bare minimum required to sustain life: Angus Maddison, 1995, *Monitoring the World Economy 1820–1992*, OECD, Paris. Specifically, in benchmark years 1, 1000, 1500, 1600 and 1700 AD, Maddison estimates annual per-capita GDP for Australia as $400 (in 1990 US dollars), which converts to about $1400 in current Australian dollars.

3 Jon Altman, 1987, *Hunter-Gatherers Today: An Aboriginal Economy in North Australia*, Australian Institute of Aboriginal Studies, Canberra, cited in Ian Keen, 2004, *Aboriginal Economy and Society: Australia at the Threshold of Colonisation*, Oxford University Press, Oxford, p. 329.

4 Keen, *Aboriginal Economy and Society*, p. 346.

5 Ibid, p. 270.

6 I am indebted to Jane Mansbridge for alerting me to this literature. For example, one study finds that the Gini for wealth inequality in a handful of hunter-gatherer populations was around 0.25, well below the level of wealth inequality observed in any capitalist economy today. See Eric Alden Smith et al., 2010, 'Wealth Transmission and Inequality among Hunter-Gatherers', *Current Anthropology*, Vol. 51, No. 1, pp. 19–34 (and the many studies cited therein). One analysis contrasts egalitarianism in these societies with the jostling for power in chimpanzee societies, and points to the many mechanisms (including teasing and ridicule) used by early human societies to maintain egalitarianism: Kent Flannery and Joyce Marcus, 2012, *The Creation of Inequality: How Our Prehistoric Ancestors Set the Stage for Monarchy, Slavery and Empire*, Harvard University Press, Cambridge, MA.

7 See for example Ian Keen, 2006, 'Constraints on the Development of Enduring Inequalities in Late Holocene Australia', *Current Anthropology*, Vol. 47, No. 1, pp. 7–38. In terms of inequality of power, there have been debates in the literature over the existence of 'chiefs', and the power inequities associated with polygyny. For example, Ian Keen draws my attention to the following works: Frederick Rose, 1960, *Classification of Kin, Age Structure and Marriage among the Groote Eylandt Aborigines: A Study in Method and a Theory of Australian Kinship*, Akademie, Berlin; Ken Maddock, 1982, *The Australian Aborigines: A Portrait of Their Society*, second edition, Penguin, Ringwood, Vic; Ian Keen, 1989, 'Aboriginal Governance', in Jon Altman and Francesca Merlan (eds), *Emergent Inequalities among Contemporary Australian Aborigines*, Oceania Monographs, Sydney, pp. 17–42.

8 This is also true of modern-day Australia.

9 An account of the Tiwi people also recorded several instances of men with more than twenty wives: see Charles Hart and Arnold Pilling, 1960, *The Tiwi of North Australia*, Holt, New York, p. 17.

10 Naturally, men could not entirely control their partners' sexual behaviours (particularly in instances where men had large numbers of wives), but any such liaisons would likely be considered illicit by others in the community.

11 Robert Hughes, 1988, *The Fatal Shore*, Vintage, Sydney, p. 96. In terms of food, Hughes reports that male convicts got two-thirds of the allowance given to soldiers, and female convicts got two-thirds of that amount. I am grateful to Rob Bray for reminding me of this account.

12 The estimate (by Mark Thomas) is that the top 10 per cent in 1790 had 24 per cent of total income. To put it into perspective, the top 10 per cent share from 1941 to 2010 ranged between 34 per cent and 25 per cent. Thomas suggests that valuing goods at British prices is the more appropriate measure, so this is the one I present here. He also points out that this approach is unable to account for differences in imputed rent. See Mark Thomas, 1991, 'The Evolution of Inequality in Australia in the Nineteenth Century', in Y.S. Brenner, Hartmut Kaelble and Mark Thomas (eds), *Income Distribution in Historical Perspective*, Cambridge University Press, Cambridge, pp. 149–173.

13 Peter Lindert and Jeff Williamson estimate that in the late eighteenth century, the top 10 per cent had 31 per cent of income in the United States, 45–49 per cent of income in England and Wales, and 51 per cent of income in the Netherlands. See Peter H. Lindert and Jeffrey G. Williamson, 2012, 'American Incomes 1774–1860', National Bureau of Economic Research Working Paper No. 18396, NBER, Cambridge, MA.

14 For a comparable dataset of top 10 per cent income shares, see Andrew Leigh, 2007, 'How Closely Do Top Income Shares Track Other Measures of Inequality?', *Economic Journal*, Vol. 117, No. 524, pp. F619–F633. A wide range of historic inequality estimates are also contained in Branko Milanovic, Peter H. Lindert and Jeffrey G. Williamson, 2011, 'Pre-Industrial Inequality', *Economic Journal*, Vol. 121, pp. 255–272.

15 One way to see the low living standards of early British colonisers is to note that Maddison's estimate of per-capita GDP in Australia is $400 in 1700 and

$518 in 1820 (both figures are 1990 US dollars, from Maddison, *Monitoring the World Economy 1820–1992* (see note 2, Chapter 1)).

16 Recounted in Watkin Tench, 1793, *A Complete Account of the Settlement at Port Jackson in New South Wales*, G. Nicol and J. Sewell, London. I am grateful to John Hirst for drawing my attention to this delicious morsel of Australian history.

17 Thomas, 'The Evolution of Inequality in Australia in the Nineteenth Century' (see note 12, Chapter 1), pp. 149–173.

18 This table presents results compiled by Mark Thomas, 'The Evolution of Inequality' (see note 12, Chapter 1), pp. 149–173. Note that Grose and Paterson were colonial administrators in the interregnum between governors. Thomas's research also omits Governor William Bligh (who served from 1806 to 1808) and the interregnum governors who served in the years 1808 and 1809.

19 Thomas, 'The Evolution of Inequality' (see note 12, Chapter 1), pp. 149–173.

20 William D. Rubinstein, 2004, *The All-Time Australian 200 Rich List*, Allen and Unwin, Crows Nest, NSW.

21 Being in the last two decades of life or on the *BRW* rich list are not as different as they might seem. For example, on the 2012 rich list, there were more people aged over eighty than under fifty: John Stensholt, 2012, 'Portrait of Rich Change: Ageing Fortunes', *Australian Financial Review*, 26–27 May, pp. 50–51.

22 Charles Darwin, 1879, *A Naturalist's Voyage*, p. 444, quoted in Hirst, *The Australians* (see note 1, Introduction), p. 99.

23 Thomas, 'The Evolution of Inequality' (see note 12, Chapter 1), pp. 149–173.

24 Peter H. Lindert and Jeffrey G. Williamson, 2003, 'Does Globalization Make the World More Unequal?', in Michael D. Bordo, Alan M. Taylor and Jeffrey G. Williamson (eds), *Globalization in Historical Perspective*, University of Chicago Press, Chicago, p. 237. To be precise, Williamson's measure compares wages to rents, since both are flows (but because he derives Australian rents from land prices, the practical result is similar). This measure is most applicable to an era when landownership is relatively concentrated (and thus the typical unskilled worker is a renter rather than a landowner).

25 Because the average number of working days per week and annual leave per year has changed over time, I simply ignore weekends and public holidays. Instead, I calculate daily wages by dividing weekly wages by seven, or annual wages by 365. Needless to say, the comparisons would remain unchanged if a different divisor was used instead. Average weekly ordinary time earnings for full-time adults were $1889 in November 2023, according to Australian Bureau of Statistics, 2024, *Average Weekly Earnings*, ABS, Canberra. Farmland price is the 2023 estimate in the ABARES Farmland Price Index, published on the website of the Australian Bureau of Agricultural and Resource Economics and Sciences.

26 Laura Panza and Jeffrey Williamson, 2019, 'Australian squatters, convicts, and capitalists: dividing up a fast-growing frontier pie, 1821–71', *Economic History Review*, vol. 72, no. 2, pp. 568–594. Their analysis covers New South Wales (including what would become Victoria and Queensland) from 1828

to 1860, and all of Australia except Western Australia and Queensland from 1861 to 1871.

27 Quoted in Geoffrey Bolton, 1990, *The Oxford History of Australia, Volume 5: 1942–1988, The Middle Way*, Oxford University Press, Melbourne, p. 289.

28 Because land prices are not available for all of Australia back to the 1860s, I focus on Victoria. Wage series are from Wray Vamplew (ed.), 1987, *Australians: Historical Statistics*, Fairfax, Syme & Weldon Associates, Broadway, NSW. I use 'Average Annual Earnings in Manufacturing, Victoria' (LAB-182, p. 160) for 1865–1900 and 'Average Annual Male Earnings in Manufacturing, Victoria' (LAB-196, p. 161) for 1909–1939 and 1944–1950. Missing years are linearly interpolated, and weekends are ignored (i.e. daily wages are 1/365th of annual wages). Land price series also cover Victoria, and are from Alan Taylor, 1992, 'The Value of Land in Australia Before 1913', Source Papers in Economic History, No. 19, ANU, Table 10 (Column 1) for 1865–1913; and Robert H. Scott, 1969, 'The Value of Land in Australia', Working Paper, Reserve Bank of Australia, Sydney, pp. 55 and 57 (Vic. Columns) for 1914–1950. The Scott series are scaled down by a factor of 0.818, being the ratio of the two series in 1901–1913. Nineteenth-century wage estimates are more contested than land prices, but I am satisfied that my estimates use the most accurate available data and are consistent with estimates published by Diane Hutchinson at *Measuring Worth* (measuringworth.com). See also detailed breakdowns in Ahmed Fahour and Glenn Withers, 'Australian Wages 1850–1900', unpublished working paper.

29 This trend was not unique to Victoria. Martin Shanahan and John Wilson estimate wage rate to land price ratios for four colonies/states: Victoria (1865–1913), South Australia (1862–1913), New South Wales (1883–1913) and Queensland (1881–1913). Each of these estimates shows a rise in inequality over the period for which data are available. See Martin Shanahan and John Wilson, 2007, 'Measuring Inequality Trends in Colonial Australia Using Factor-Price Ratios: The Importance of Boundaries', *Australian Economic History Review*, Vol. 47, No. 1, pp. 6–21.

30 Laura Panza and Jeffrey Williamson, 2021, 'Always egalitarian? Australian earnings inequality 1870–1910', *Australian Economic History Review*, vol. 61, no. 2, pp. 228–246.

31 Trollope visited Australia in 1871 and 1875, and his words are cited in Russel Ward, 2012 [1958], 'The Australian Legend', extracted in Robert Manne and Chris Feik (eds), *The Words That Made Australia: How a Nation Came to Know Itself*, Black Inc., Melbourne.

32 Stuart Macintyre, 1986, *The Oxford History of Australia, Volume 4: 1901–1942, The Succeeding Age*, Oxford University Press, Melbourne, pp. 1–22.

33 Frank Hardy, 2000 [1950], *Power without Glory*, Random House, Milsons Point, p. 24.

34 Barry Higman, 2002, *Domestic Service in Australia*, Melbourne University Press, Melbourne, p. 20.

35 Higman compares the share of the population working as domestic servants with the share for the United Kingdom and United States.

Throughout this period, Australia has a smaller share of people in domestic servitude than the United Kingdom. Interestingly, however, we had a larger share than the United States until the mid-1930s, after which the United States has had a larger share than Australia. See Higman, *Domestic Service in Australia* (see note 34, Chapter 1), p. 25.

36 John Hirst, 2009, *Sense and Nonsense in Australian History*, Black Inc., Melbourne, pp. 145–173.

37 Henry Lawson, 1900, 'For'ard', *In the Days When the World Was Wide*, Angus and Robertson, Sydney.

Chapter 2

1 W.K. Hancock, 2012 [1930], 'The Australian Democracy', extracted in *The Words That Made Australia* (see note 31, Chapter 1), p. 47.

2 Edmund Barton, *Commonwealth Parliamentary Debates*, 26 September 1901, p. 5233.

3 This paragraph draws on Rubinstein, *The All-Time Australian 200 Rich List* (see note 20, Chapter 1).

4 McKay had until this point been paying his workers six shillings a day. For a useful analysis of the Harvester judgment, see Joe Isaac, 2008, 'The Economic Consequences of Harvester', *Australian Economic History Review*, Vol. 48, No. 3, pp. 280–300.

5 See Andrew Baker, '100 Years of Rugby League: From the Great Divide to the Super Era', *The Independent*, 20 August 1995. A similar split had taken place in the United Kingdom twelve years earlier: see Tony Collins, 1998, *Rugby's Great Split: Class, Culture, and the Origins of Rugby League Football*, Frank Cass, London.

6 Collins, *Rugby's Great Split* (see note 5, Chapter 2), p. 224; 'Dr. H.V. Evatt', 1930, *Canberra Times*. 19 December. p. 1.

7 Diane Hutchinson, 2012, 'Weekly Wages, Average Compensation and Minimum Wage for Australia from 1861–Present', *Measuring Worth* (measuringworth.com).

8 Macintyre, *The Oxford History of Australia, Volume 4* (see note 32, Chapter 1), pp. 220–21.

9 Census figures on housing construction in 1911 and 1921 are reported in R. Jackson and Helen Bridge, 1987, 'Housing', in *Australians: Historical Statistics* (see note 28, Chapter 1), pp. 350–51.

10 Macintyre, *The Oxford History of Australia, Volume 4* (see note 27, Chapter 1), pp. 145–46.

11 Ibid., p. 163.

12 Ibid., p. 194.

13 Ibid., p. 221.

14 Corrado Gini, 1914, 'Sulla misura della concentrazione e della reitbart`a dei caratteri', *Atti del Reale Istituto Veneto di Scienze, Lettere ed Arti*, Vol. 73, Part II, pp. 1203–1248. Translated into English by Giovanni Maria Giorgi, and republished as Corrado Gini, 2005, 'On the Measurement of Concentration and Variability of Characters', *METRON – International Journal of Statistics*, Vol. 63, No. 1, pp. 3–38.

15 The sources for Figure 4 are Richard Burkhauser, Markus Hahn and Roger Wilkins, 'Measuring Top Incomes Using Tax Record Data: A Cautionary Tale from Australia', *Journal of Economic Inequality*, Vol. 13, No. 2, 2015, pp. 181–205 and Anthony B. Atkinson and Andrew Leigh, 'The Distribution of Top Incomes in Australia', *Economic Record*, Vol. 83, No. 262, 2007, pp. 247–61. The most famous use of taxation statistics to estimate inequality was Simon Kuznets's work in the 1950s, but Thomas Piketty's top income estimates for France were the first to use external control totals for population and personal income. This means that the estimates are not affected by changes in the share of the population that are taxpayers.

16 The 1950–51 tax year was extremely unusual. For example, 90 per cent of those with taxable incomes over £20,000 were farmers: H.P. Brown, 1957, 'Estimation of Income Distribution in Australia', in M. Gilbert and R. Stone (eds) *Income and Wealth: Series VI*, Bowes and Bowes, London, pp. 202–38.

17 Real GDP fell by 8 per cent from 1929–30 to 1930–31: Macintyre, *The Oxford History of Australia, Volume 4* (see note 32, Chapter 1), p. 254.

18 Ibid., pp. 261, 270.

19 J.R. Robertson, 1974, '1930–39', in F.K. Crowley (ed.), *A New History of Australia*, William Heinemann, Melbourne, pp. 415–57.

20 Hutchinson, 'Weekly Wages' (see note 7, Chapter 2).

21 Quoted in John Edwards, 2005, *Curtin's Gift: Reinterpreting Australia's Greatest Prime Minister*, Allen and Unwin, Crows Nest, NSW, p. 124. Edwards argues that Curtin was responsible for uniform taxation, modern banking, the full employment policy and engagement with the international economy (via the GATT, IMF and World Bank); and that he oversaw the beginning of Commonwealth support for university education, Commonwealth housing and major changes to social security.

22 Clothing and meat rationing was only abolished in 1948, while butter and tea rationing continued until 1950: Bolton, *The Oxford History of Australia, Volume 5* (see note 27, Chapter 1), p. 61.

23 Commonwealth of Australia, 1945, *Full Employment in Australia*, Australian Government, Canberra.

24 Bolton, *The Oxford History of Australia, Volume 5* (see note 27, Chapter 1), p. 34.

25 Ibid., p. 32 (houses) and p. 75 (cars).

26 Ibid., p. 99. The first Australian Holden cars rolled off the production line in 1948.

27 An income question did not become a regular part of the Australian census until 1976. Note that the 1943 census was only a partial census, and results are based on matching taxation returns in 1942–43 with the partial census (using identity card numbers). For details, see Brown, 'Estimation of Income Distribution in Australia' (see note 16, Chapter 2), pp. 202–238; Peter Saunders, 1993, 'Longer Run Changes in the Distribution of Income in Australia', *Economic Record*, Vol. 69, No. 207, pp. 353–66.

28 For example, one study reports the male Gini coefficient as being 0.43 in 1914–15, 0.49 in 1932–33, 0.41 in 1942–43, 0.34 in 1968–69, 0.35 in 1978–79 and 0.36 in 1980–81: Saunders, 'Longer Run Changes' (see note 27,

Chapter 2), pp. 353–366. See also Brown, 'Estimation of Income Distribution in Australia' (see note 16. Chapter 2), pp. 202–238; Frank Jones, 1975, 'The Changing Shape of the Australian Income Distribution, 1914–15 and 1968–9', *Australian Economic History Review*, Vol. 15, pp. 21–34; Ian McLean and Sue Richardson, 1986, 'More or Less Equal? Australian Income Distribution in 1933 and 1980', *Economic Record*, Vol. 62, pp. 67–81.

29 Noel G. Butlin, 1983, 'Trends in Australian Income Distribution: A First Glance', Australian National University Working Paper in Economic History No. 17, ANU, Canberra. Other studies to look at long-run changes in unskilled/skilled wage ratios include Keith Hancock and K. Moore, 1972, 'The Occupational Wage Structure in Australia Since 1914', *British Journal of Industrial Relations*, Vol. 10, No. 1, pp. 107–22; C. Forster and P. Harris, 1983, 'A Note on Engineering Wages in Melbourne 1892–1929', *Australian Economic History Review*, Vol. 23, No. 1, pp. 50–57; J.E. Isaac, 1965, 'Wage Drift in the Australian Metal Industries', *Economic Record*, Vol. 41, No. 94, pp. 145–72.

30 Bolton, *The Oxford History of Australia, Volume 5* (see note 27, Chapter 1), p. 33.

31 See ABS, 1988, 'History of Pensions and Other Benefits in Australia', *Year Book*, Cat. No. 1301.0, ABS, Canberra.

32 Bolton, *The Oxford History of Australia, Volume 5* (see note 27, Chapter 1), p. 103.

33 Donald Horne, 1980, *Time of Hope: Australia 1966–72*, Angus and Robertson, Sydney, p. 88.

34 Mike Pottenger and Andrew Leigh, 2016, 'Long-Run Trends in Australian Executive Remuneration: BHP, 1887–2012', *Australian Economic History Review*, Vol. 56, No. 1, pp. 2–20. during this period, our estimates are based on combining unofficial estimates with published estimates of directors' remuneration.

35 Bolton, *The Oxford History of Australia, Volume 5* (see note 27, Chapter 1), p. 90.

36 For example, the NSW government granted workers three weeks' annual leave in 1958.

37 Craig McGregor, 1966, *Profile of Australia*, Hodder and Stoughton, London, p. 310.

38 From 1942 to 1978, I found that the pre-tax Gini coefficient fell by nine points, from 0.35 to 0.26: Andrew Leigh, 2005, 'Deriving Long-Run Inequality Series from Tax Data', *Economic Record*, Vol. 81, No. S1, pp. S58–S70. On a post-tax basis, the male Gini coefficient in Australia fell from 0.24 to 0.18. Extending the series to 2010, I estimate a pre-tax Gini of 0.36 and a post-tax Gini of 0.31 (both higher than in 1942).

39 A nine-point difference in the Gini is what today separates Australia from the more equal Scandinavian countries (or in the opposite direction, from the more unequal Latin American countries): OECD, 2011, 'Income Inequality', in *OECD Factbook 2011–2012: Economic, Environmental and Social Statistics*, OECD Publishing, Paris, p. 81.

40 Gender pay gaps narrowed through the post-war decades, but the equal pay cases were important because the 1969 decision determined that women's

award wages must be at least 85 per cent of men's award wages, while the 1972 decision determined that men's and women's award wages must be equal.

41 Rubinstein, *The All-Time Australian 200 Rich List* (see note 20, Chapter 1), p. 139.
42 Ibid., p. 143.
43 Quoted in Hirst, *Sense and Nonsense in Australian History* (see note 36, Chapter 1), p. 172.
44 McGregor, *Profile of Australia* (see note 37, Chapter 2), pp. 93 and 97. McGregor also notes that a similar share of Australians (55 per cent) self-described as 'middle class' in 1949.
45 Quoted in ibid., p. 93.
46 Ward, 'The Australian Legend' (see note 31, Chapter 1).
47 Anthony B. Atkinson and Andrew Leigh, 2007, 'Top Incomes in New Zealand 1921–2005: Understanding the Effects of Marginal Tax Rates, Migration Threat and the Macroeconomy', *Review of Income and Wealth*, Vol. 54, No. 2, pp. 149–65.
48 Lucas Chancel, Thomas Piketty, Emmanuel Saez and Gabriel Zucman, *World Inequality Report 2022* (note 33), pp. 93, 166–67.
49 Facundo Alvaredo, Lucas Chancel, Thomas Piketty, Emmanuel Saez and Gabriel Zucman, 2018, *World Inequality Report 2018*, Harvard University Press, Cambridge, p. 241.
50 Peter Turchin, 2023, *End Times: Elites, Counter-Elites and the Path of Political Disintegration*, Penguin, New York.
51 Claudia Goldin and Robert Margo, 1992, 'The Great Compression: The Wage Structure in the United States at Mid-Century', *Quarterly Journal of Economics*, Vol. 107, No. 1, pp. 1–34; Claudia Goldin and Larry Katz, 2001, 'Decreasing (and Then Increasing) Inequality in America: A Tale of Two Half Centuries', in Finis Welch, *The Causes and Consequences of Increasing Inequality*, University of Chicago Press, Chicago, pp. 37–82.
52 Simon Kuznets, 1955, 'Economic Growth and Income Inequality', *American Economic Review*, Vol. 45, pp. 1–28; John K. Galbraith, 1958, *The Affluent Society*, Hamish Hamilton, London, p. 2.
53 Henry J. Aaron, 1978, *Politics and the Professors*, Brookings Institution, Washington DC, p. 17.
54 In his book on meritocracy, US writer Christopher Hayes argues that the areas where the left has done best over the past generation (for example, equality for same-sex couples, reducing racial discrimination and increasing the representation of women in parliament) are those for which a strong meritocratic argument can be made. Conversely, he says, the areas on which the left has done worst (for example, maintaining high levels of union membership, progressive taxes and low inequality) are those that are less amenable to meritocratic arguments: Christopher Hayes, 2012, *Twilight of the Elites: America after Meritocracy*, Crown, New York, p. 47.
55 As the ABS notes: 'The changes to the Constitution meant that all Aboriginal and Torres Strait Islander people should be counted in the Census. In the 1966 Census, an attempt had been made to achieve as

full a coverage as possible. However, following the 1967 Referendum, a more concerted effort could be made within the new legal framework, starting from the 1971 Census.': ABS, 2011, 'Aboriginal and Torres Strait Islander Peoples and the Census after the 1967 Referendum', *Reflecting a Nation: Stories from the 2011 Census*, Cat. No. 2071.0, ABS, Canberra.

56 On 'protection all round', see Andrew Leigh, 2002, 'Trade Liberalisation and the Australian Labor Party', *Australian Journal of Politics and History*, Vol. 48, No. 4, pp. 487–508. The words 'two Wongs don't make a White' were said by Arthur Calwell, *House of Representatives Hansard*, 2 December 1947. Although Calwell was making a quip about a member of parliament with the last name 'White', his racial views do seem to reflect the discriminatory attitudes of the time. For example, Calwell wrote in 1972: 'any man who tries to stigmatize the Australian community as racist because they want to preserve this country for the white race is doing our nation great harm ... I reject, in conscience, the idea that Australia should or ever can become a multi-racial society and survive' (Arthur Calwell, 1972, *Be Just and Fear Not*, Lloyd O'Neil in association with Rigby, Hawthorn, Vic).

57 Compared with the OECD 20 (the twenty members in the Organisation for Economic Cooperation and Development in 1961), Australia's real per-capita GDP growth rate was 1.3 percentage points slower in the 1950s, 0.6 percentage points slower in the 1960s and 0.9 percentage points slower in the 1970s: Australian Government, 2012, *Australia in the Asian Century White Paper*, Australian Government, Canberra, p. 82. Others place less emphasis on the closed economy as a drag on Australia's economic growth, arguing instead that Australia could have been expected to grow more slowly than other advanced nations in this period, because we started at a higher level of affluence: see, for example, Steve Dowrick, 1993, 'Australia's Long-Run Macroeconomic Performance', in Stephen King and Peter Lloyd (eds) *Economic Rationalism: Dead End or Way Forward*, Allen and Unwin, St Leonards, NSW, pp. 236–57; and Steve Dowrick and Duc-Tho Nguyen, 1989, 'OECD Comparative Economic Growth 1950–85: Catch-Up and Convergence', *American Economic Review*, Vol. 79, pp. 1010–30.

58 This account draws upon Geoffrey Blainey and Ann G. Smith, 'Lewis, Essington (1881–1961)', *Australian Dictionary of Biography*, National Centre of Biography, Australian National University (adb.anu.edu.au/biography/lewis-essington-7185/text12419).

59 Blainey and Smith, 'Lewis, Essington (1881–1961)'.

60 Salary from Blainey and Smith, 'Lewis, Essington (1881–1961)'. Average wages compiled by Hutchinson, 'Weekly Wages' (see Note 7, Chapter 2).

61 Lewis's estate value is from Blainey and Smith, 'Lewis, Essington (1881–1961)' (see Note 7, Chapter 2). Average wages compiled by Hutchinson, 'Weekly Wages' (see Note 7, Chapter 2).

62 Mike Henry's total remuneration in 2023 was US$13.7 million, which converts to A$20.4 million at the time of writing. Average ordinary time earnings for full time adults in Australia in November 2023 were $98,000. The ratio of BHP CEO pay to average earnings has been at this level for

some time. For example, Marius Kloppers (BHP's CEO from 2009 to 2013) earned between 180 and 270 times the average Australian wage in every year of his tenure: Pottenger and Leigh, 'Long-Run Trends in Australian Executive Remuneration' (see note 34, Chapter 2).

Chapter 3

1 Elisabeth Wynhausen, 2005, *Dirt Cheap: Life at the Wrong End of the Job Market*, Macmillan, Sydney, p. 78.

2 Andrew Leigh, 2022, 'Tackling Inequality: Lessons from the Postwar Reconstruction' in David Lowe, Lyndon Megarrity and Carolyn Holbrook (eds), *Lessons from History: Leading Historians Tackle Australia's Greatest Challenges*, NewSouth Books, Sydney.

3 These figures are from the Employee Earnings and Hours survey. For comparability, they cover full-time adult non-managerial employees. Figures are reported on a weekly basis, but I have converted these to annual wages for comparability with most of the other figures in the chapter. I am indebted to Rob Bray and Peter Whiteford for their assistance in obtaining earlier years' data. For an analysis of earnings inequality from 1975 to 2014, see Jeff Borland and Michael Coelli, 2016, 'Labour market inequality in Australia', *Economic Record*, vol. 92, no. 299, pp. 517–47.

4 Australian Taxation Statistics, 2023, *Taxation Statistics 2020–21*, Table 15A, ATO, Canberra.

5 For 1990s trends, see Productivity Commission, 2009, *Executive Remuneration in Australia*, Report No. 49, Final Inquiry Report, Melbourne, p. 49. To chart trends for the period 2001–2022, I use reported pay figures, since my source does not estimate realised pay prior to 2014. The reported pay figures are median reported pay among ASX 100 CEOs, sourced from Australian Council of Superannuation Investors, 2023, *CEO Pay in ASX 200 Companies: July 2023*, ACSI, Melbourne, p.34. Median earnings of full-time employees are sourced from the Australian Bureau of Statistics *Employee Earnings and Hours* survey (2001 is $39,000, being the average of 2000 and 2002; 2022 is $85,540, being the average of 2021 and 2023).

6 Realised pay is defined as the value of cash and equity actually received by top CEOs, and is sourced from Australian Council of Superannuation Investors, *CEO Pay in ASX 200 Companies: July 2023* (see note 5, Chapter 3), p. 7.

7 Productivity Commission, *Executive Remuneration in Australia* (see note 5, Chapter 3), pp. 54–55; Australian Council of Superannuation Investors, *CEO Pay in ASX 200 Companies: July 2023* (see note 5, Chapter 3).

8 Productivity Commission, *Executive Remuneration in Australia* (see note 5, Chapter 3), p. 74.

9 Gideon Haigh notes one such example: 'Thanks to an option plan in which the only performance hurdle was that shareholder return based on price and dividends exceed 10 per cent per annum compounded, Peter Smedley made A$20 million on bundling up and flogging the financial conglomerate Colonial'. See Gideon Haigh, 2003, *Bad Company: The Cult of the CEO*, Quarterly Essay 10, Black Inc., Melbourne, p. 50.

10 Australian Council of Superannuation Investors, *CEO Pay in ASX 200 Companies: July 2023*, (see note 5, Chapter 3), p.22 (Qantas's Alan Joyce, the only ASX 100 CEO to receive zero bonus, nonetheless received a two-year retention equity allocation, potentially worth over $4 million).
11 During 1989–2007, the ASX as a whole grew by approximately 680 per cent in real terms (using the GDP deflator). Over the same period, the average real growth rate (unweighted) for the top twenty firms was 1437 per cent. Since some firms were not listed for the full period, this likely understates the growth rate of the largest companies. See Productivity Commission, *Executive Remuneration in Australia* (see note 5. Chapter 3), p. 56. The change suggests that this was an era in which the returns to scale increased, perhaps because shifts in technology and distribution models advantaged incumbent players in the telecommunications and banking sectors. Ironically, this is a case of inequality in the share market (more rapid growth at the top) driving more inequality in the labour market.
12 In 1947, federal backbench MPs earned five times the average wage. In 1950, puisne High Court Justices earned eleven times the average wage. Salaries of parliamentarians and judges are taken from Anthony B. Atkinson and Andrew Leigh, 2007, 'The Distribution of Top Incomes in Australia', *Economic Record*, Vol. 83, No. 262, pp. 247–261, updated with 2012 figures from the Remuneration Tribunal website. Note, however, that I use a different average wage series than Atkinson and Leigh, being Hutchinson, 'Weekly Wages' (see note 7, Chapter 2). This does not affect the trends.
13 The 2012 increase in the salaries of federal MPs was also accompanied by the abolition of certain benefits (for example, the international parliamentary study tour), which were not included in the base pay.
14 Figures including and excluding capital gains are from Richard Burkhauser, Markus Hahn and Roger Wilkins, 2015, 'Measuring Top Incomes Using Tax Record Data: A Cautionary Tale from Australia', *Journal of Economic Inequality*, Vol. 13, No. 2, pp. 181–205.
15 Nicolas Hérault, Dean Hyslop, Stephen Jenkins and Roger Wilkins, 2024, 'Rising top-income persistence in Australia: Evidence from income tax data', *Review of Income and Wealth*, forthcoming.
16 US estimates are for 1980–2022, including capital gains, sourced from the World Inequality Database (https://wid.world). The income threshold to enter the US top 1 per cent in 2020 was US$478,423 (approximately A$720,000), while the threshold to enter the top 1 per cent in Australia was $275,245, less than half as much.
17 Miranda Stewart, Sarah Voitchovsky and Roger Wilkins, 2017, 'Women and top incomes in Australia', in Miranda Stewart (ed.) *Tax, Social Policy and Gender: Rethinking Equality and Efficiency*, ANU Press, Canberra, pp, 257–91.
18 David Richardson and Matt Grudnoff, 2023, 'Inequality on Steroids: The Distribution of Economic Growth in Australia', Australia Institute, Canberra, April.
19 For example, Peter Whiteford presents annual household income measures which show an increase in the Gini coefficient across all households from 0.27 in 1981–82 to 0.34 in 2009–10: Peter Whiteford, 2012, 'Inequality and

Redistribution in the Australian Welfare State', research supported as part of the GINI project, 'Growing Inequalities' Impacts', Presentation at NATSEM, Canberra, 3 October 2012. Similarly, Rob Bray presents estimates of equivalised disposable income inequality that show a rise in the Gini from 0.29 in 1990 to 0.33 in 2010 (using the Survey of Income and Housing), and from 0.29 in 1976 to 0.32 in 2010 (using the Household Expenditure Survey, excluding records with negative and zero amounts). Using the Household, Income and Labour Dynamics in Australia (HILDA) survey, Bray finds no increase in the Gini coefficient over 2001–2010, except where he uses a balanced panel: J. Rob Bray, 2012, 'Changes in Inequality in Australia and the Redistributional Impact of Taxes and Government Benefits', Paper presented at an ASSA and Crawford School Roundtable on Economic Growth and Wellbeing, ANU, Canberra, 21–22 November 2012. My own estimates of the male Gini (combining taxation and census data) are that over the period 1980–2000, it rose from 0.28 to 0.38 (pre-tax) or 0.20 to 0.28 (post-tax): see Andrew Leigh, 2005, 'Deriving Long-Run Inequality Series from Tax Data', *Economic Record*, Vol. 81, pp. S58–S70. Updating the series from 2000 to 2010, I estimate that the pre-tax male Gini has fallen to 0.36, and the post-tax male Gini has risen to 0.31. See also OECD, 2011, *Divided We Stand: Why Inequality Keeps Rising*, OECD, Paris; OECD, 2008, *Growing Unequal? Income Distribution and Poverty in OECD Countries*, OECD: Paris; Frank Stilwell and Kirrily Jordan, 2007, *Who Gets What? Analysing Economic Inequality in Australia*, Cambridge University Press, Melbourne; Fred Argy, 2006, 'Equality of Opportunity in Australia: Myth and Reality', Discussion Paper 85, the Australia Institute, Canberra; Peter Saunders, 2005, *The Poverty Wars*, UNSW Press, Sydney; Fred Argy, 2003, *Where To From Here?: Australian Egalitarianism Under Threat*, Allen and Unwin, Crows Nest, NSW; Denise Doiron, 2012, 'Income Inequality: A Review of Recent Trends and Issues', Fay Gale Lecture 2011, Academy of the Social Sciences in Australia, Academy Proceedings 2/2012.

20 Peter Whiteford, 2013, 'Australia: Inequality and Prosperity and Their Impacts in a Radical Welfare State', H.C. Coombs Policy Forum, Discussion Paper, p. 39. Another study has attempted to include 'in-kind' benefits, and concluded that health care spending is mildly progressive, while education spending is mildly regressive (since higher income households are more likely to have dependent children). Taken together, health and education spending have a modest equalising effect on household income inequality. See Jared Greenville, Clinton Pobke and Nikki Rogers, 2013, *Trends in the Distribution of Income in Australia*, Productivity Commission Staff Working Paper, Canberra, p. 87.

21 I have been unable to locate a single authoritative study on relative poverty over the past forty years, but fortunately a fairly consistent picture emerges from studies covering shorter timespans. See Peter Saunders, 1996, 'Poverty and Deprivation in Australia', *Year Book Australia*, Cat. No. 1301.0, ABS, Canberra, Table S2.6 (showing an increase from 1972–73 to 1989–90); Roger Wilkins, 2007, 'The Changing Socio-Demographic Composition of Poverty in Australia: 1982 to 2004', *Australian Journal of Social Issues*, Vol. 42, No. 4,

pp. 481–501, Fig. 1 (showing an increase from 1981–82 to 2002–03); Roger Wilkins, 2012, 'Do We Really Know What Happened to Income Inequality in Australia over the Last Decade?', Parliamentary Library Vital Issues Seminar, 10 October 2012 (showing an increase from 1993–94 to 2009–10). An exception to these findings is a study that uses expenditure surveys (rather than income surveys) and finds a larger percentage increase in bottom quintile incomes than top quintile incomes from 1984 to 2009–10: see Ben Phillips, Jinjing Li and Matthew Taylor, 2012, *Prices These Days! The Cost of Living in Australia*, AMP.NATSEM Income and Wealth Report, No. 31, AMP, Sydney. From conversations with lead author Ben Phillips, this appears to be entirely driven by an extremely large change (32 per cent) in bottom quintile incomes from 1984 to 1988. Excluding the 1984 survey, Phillips's study finds – in common with other research – an increase in inequality from 1988 to 2009–10. Given the relatively small sample in the 1984 survey, Phillips's own view is that the income surveys should be preferred to expenditure surveys when analysing income inequality. For the period 2001–2022, the definitive study is J. Rob Bray, 2024, 'Relative Income Poverty: Levels, Trends, Context and Issues', Working Paper, Centre for Social Policy Research, Australian National University, Canberra (Bray's estimate of a 13 per cent poverty rate is for 2022).

22 Measures of consumption inequality tend to be lower than measures of income inequality because the poor often borrow and the rich often save. Rob Bray's analysis of the Household Expenditure Survey finds an increase in the Gini coefficient for consumption from 1976 to 2010. However, the rise is only 0.7 Gini points if all housing costs are excluded, or 1.4 Gini points if housing capital repayments are included in consumption: J. Rob Bray, 2012, 'Changes in Inequality in Australia and the Redistributional Impact of Taxes and Government Benefits', Paper presented at an ASSA and Crawford School Roundtable on Economic Growth and Wellbeing, ANU, Canberra, 21–22 November 2012, pp. 24–25. Earlier studies have reached similar conclusions: see Garry Barrett, Thomas Crossley and Christopher Worswick, 2000, 'Consumption and Income Inequality in Australia', *Economic Record*, Vol. 76, No. 233, pp. 116–138. Related to this is the argument that inequality was a key cause of the over-borrowing that underpinned the US sub-prime mortgage crisis: Raghuram Rajan, 2010, *Fault Lines: How Hidden Fractures Still Threaten the World Economy*, Princeton University Press, Princeton, NJ.

23 For example, US household income (in 2022 dollars) at the tenth percentile was US$11,770 in 1967, and US$17,100 in 2022: Gloria Guzman and Melissa Kollar, 2023, *US Census Bureau, Current Population Reports, P60-279, Income in the United States: 2022*, US Government Publishing Office, Washington, DC, September, p. 32.

24 Employment calculations are based on the 2021 HILDA survey. On the increasing spatial concentration of unemployment, see Bob Gregory and Boyd Hunter, 1995, 'The Macro Economy and the Growth of Ghettos and Urban Poverty in Australia', CEPR Discussion Papers 325, Centre for Economic Policy Research, ANU, Canberra. On the rise in jobless

households, see Peter Dawkins, Paul Gregg and Rosanna Scutella, 2002, 'The Growth of Jobless Households in Australia', *Australian Economic Review*, Vol. 35, No. 2, pp. 133–54.

25 See Higman, *Domestic Service in Australia* (see note 34, Chapter 1), p. 25.

26 One US real-estate tycoon has six full-time household staff (three gardeners, a cleaner, a personal assistant and a household manager), plus about 200 vendors who regularly come to the house to do everything from fixing the French taps to aerating the pool: Robert Frank, 2007, *Richistan: A Journey through the Twenty-First Century Wealth Boom and the Lives of the New Rich*, Piatkus, London, pp. 22, 32–35.

27 After conducting a wealth survey in 1915, government statistician G.H. Knibbs advocated 'a decennial census of wealth' (G.H. Knibbs, 1918, *The Private Wealth of Australia and Its Growth as Ascertained by Various Methods, Together with a Report of the War Census of 1915*, Commonwealth Bureau of Census and Statistics, Melbourne, p. 180). It would be nearly a century before the ABS began conducting regular surveys of wealth (the 'Household Wealth and Wealth Distribution' survey was first conducted in 2003–04).

28 I am grateful to Nigel Stapledon, who updated his series originally published as Nigel Stapledon, 2012, 'Trends and Cycles in Sydney and Melbourne House Prices from 1880 to 2011', *Australian Economic History Review*, Vol. 52, No. 3, pp. 293–317. Average wages are adult full-time ordinary time earnings, as reported in Australian Bureau of Statistics, 2024, Average Weekly Earnings, ABS, Canberra, Cat No 6302.0, Table 3 for 1994–2023. To match these full-time estimates, from 1950 to 1993, I use average compensation figures from Diane Hutchinson and Florian Ploeckl, 2024, 'Weekly Wages, Average Compensation and Minimum Wage for Australia from 1861–Present', available at the Measuring Worth website. From 1880 to 1949, I use Hutchinson and Ploeckl's series of average weekly earnings for all employees. Part-time employment was less common in past generations, but to the extent that this approach affects the results, it will create a slight upwards bias in earlier years.

29 Rachel Ong ViforJ, 2022, 'More rented, more mortgaged, less owned: what the census tells us about housing', *The Conversation*, 6 July; Danielle Wood, 2023, 'Creating a better Australia for Generation Next', Giblin Lecture, Hobart, 30 August.

30 For details, see Pamela Katic and Andrew Leigh, 2013, 'Top Wealth Shares in Australia 1915–2012', *Review of Income and Wealth*, vol. 62, no. 2, pp. 209–222. Other studies of Australian wealth inequality include N. Podder and N.C. Kakwani, 1976, 'Distribution of Wealth in Australia', *Review of Income and Wealth*, Vol. 22, No. 1, pp. 75–92; John Piggott, 1984, 'The Distribution of Wealth in Australia – A Survey', *Economic Record*, Vol. 60, No. 170, pp. 252–265; Michael Schneider, 2004, *The Distribution of Wealth*, Edward Elgar, Ann Arbor, MI.

31 The use of inheritance tax records to estimate inequality dates back to the first decade of the twentieth century. Underlying this approach is that the dead are representative of the living. In effect, this approach 'blows up'

the inheritance tax distribution by multiplying it by the inverse of the mortality rate. Put another way, if death is a random sampling technique, then the inheritance tax returns can tell us about wealth inequality among the living. Implementing this approach requires tabulations that separate estates by age and gender (given that wealth differentials fan out over the life-course). Unlike previous Australian studies, Pamela Katic and I also adjust for the fact that the rich tend to outlive the poor.

32 Other surveys confirm the high levels of inequality in the early twentieth century. For example, one study estimates that between 1905 and 1915, the top 1 per cent of property owners in South Australia held 30 per cent of wealth: Martin Shanahan, 2001, 'Personal Wealth in South Australia', *Journal of Interdisciplinary History*, Vol. 32, No. 1, pp. 55–80. This was lower than the Australian average, but still far from the collaborative social model envisaged by South Australian founders Robert Gouger and Edward Wakefield: see Rob Manwaring, 2009, 'A Collaborative History of Social Innovation in South Australia', Hawke Research Institute for Sustainable Societies, University of South Australia, p. 13.

33 Recall that William Rubinstein's cut-off for the all-time Australian rich list was 0.17 per cent of GDP. There are methodological issues in comparing wealth holdings with an income cut-off, but I maintain the same approach for comparability.

34 Megan Kinninment, 2003, 'Sea Change Town Resists Change', *The Sydney Morning Herald*, 13 January.

35 As the 1988 *BRW* rich list noted: 'The sixth annual *BRW* Rich 200 reveals something that barely seemed possible in the dark days after last October's stock market crash: the rich keep getting richer – most of them anyway ... This year the aggregate wealth of the individuals and families is $24.8 billion. Last year it was $24.9 billion.' Robert Macdonald, 1988, *BRW* magazine, 2 September.

36 This approach updates the analysis in Katic and Leigh, 'Top Wealth Shares in Australia 1915–2012'(see note 30, Chapter 3).

37 The wealth share of the bottom quintile was 0.9 percent in the most recent survey: Australian Bureau of Statistics, 2022, 'Household Income and Wealth, Australia: Summary of Results, 2019–20', ABS, Canberra.

38 Lachlan Hotchin and Andrew Leigh, 2024, 'Inequality and Market Concentration: New Evidence From Australia', *Review of Income and Wealth*, forthcoming.

39 Rudolph C. and John J, Siegfried, 1992, 'How Did the Wealthiest Americans Get So Rich?', *Quarterly Review of Economics and Finance*, Vol. 32, pp. 5–26; John J,. Siegfried and Alison Roberts, 1991, 'How Did the Wealthiest Britons Get So Rich?', *Review of Industrial Organization*, Vol. 6, pp. 19–32; Tim Hazledine and John J. Siegfried, 1997, 'How Did the Wealthiest New Zealanders Get So Rich?', *New Zealand Economic Papers*, Vol. 31, No. 1, pp. 35–47. See also John J. Siegfried and David K. Round, 1994, 'How Did the Wealthiest Australians Get So Rich?' *Review of Income and Wealth*, Vol. 40, No. 2, pp. 191–204.

40 Cover image, *AFR Magazine*, 26 May 2023.

41 Australian Competition and Consumer Commission v Visy Industries Holdings Pty Limited (No 3) [2007] FCA 1617 (2 November 2007), para 320
42 The 2000 Newspoll survey asked, 'Now about the distribution of wealth across Australian society compared with ten years ago. Do you personally think that the distribution of wealth in Australia currently is more fair or less fair, or is there no difference?' Percentages omit respondents who replied that they were uncommitted.
43 Australian Council of Social Service and University of New South Wales, 2023, *Community attitudes towards poverty and inequality 2023: Snapshot report*, ACOSS and UNSW, Sydney, p. 14.
44 James MacSmith and Giselle Bueti, 2024, 'Australia's richest streets revealed', *Daily Telegraph*, 17 January.
45 An excellent multidisciplinary analysis of the lives and spending patterns of the super-rich is Iain Hay and Jonathan V. Beaverstock (eds), 2016, *Handbook on Wealth and the Super-Rich*, Edward Elgar, Cheltenham, UK.
46 Alborz Fallah, 2012, 'Vehicle Sales Figures 2011 Total', *Drive*, 5 January; Scott Collie, 2023, 'The new Porsche cars coming to Australia in 2024', *CarExpert*, 7 December. The prior decade also saw strong growth in luxury car sales. During the 2000s, Porsche sales grew by 70 percent, while Maserati sales increased fivefold: Angus Grigg, 2010, 'How Did We Get So Rich?', *Australian Financial Review*, 23–28 December, pp. 32–33.
47 Specifically, the time taken to accelerate to 100 kilometres per hour by gravity is 2.83 seconds.
48 See, for example, *Heli Biz* (helibiz.com).
49 Australia had 739 registered helicopters in 1996, 943 in 2000, 1800 in 2010 and 2386 in 2022. See Bureau of Infrastructure, Transport and Regional Economics, 2023, *Australian Aircraft Activity 2022*, Department of Infrastructure, Transport, Regional Development, Communications and the Arts, Canberra (and its predecessor publications). On the attempt to create a floating helipad on Sydney harbour, see Jonathan Swan, 2012, 'Heliport Move Reckless, Turnbull Tells O'Farrell', *The Sydney Morning Herald*, 19 December; Jonathan Swan, 2012, 'No-Fly Zone: Helipad Plan Grounded', *The Sydney Morning Herald*, 23 December.
50 Stephanie Convery, 2023, '"Yachts at the top": power, privacy and privilege in the world of Australian superyachts', *Guardian Australia*, 25 March.
51 Myriam Robin, 2023, 'Solly Lew's new private jet shelters in its hangar', *Australian Financial Review*, 26 June.
52 Fiona Harvey, 2023, ' Private jet sales likely to reach highest ever level this year, report says', *The Guardian*, 2 May; Omar Memon, 2023, 'The Top 5 Countries for Private Jet Operations', *Simple Flying*, 20 October. Additionally, Australia's private jet fleet almost tripled in the first decade of the 2000s: Lisa Allen and John Stensholt, 2011, 'The Flying High Club', *Australian Financial Review*, 1 April.
53 Palmer's total donations are based on Australian Electoral Commission data, compiled by the 'Democracy for Sale' online database. Advertising expenditure reported in Katharine Murphy, 2019, 'Clive Palmer outspends

McDonald's, Toyota and Coles to advertise his political party', *The Guardian*, 16 August.

54 For example, the price of a 1971 Penfolds Grange has increased thirteen-fold over the past three decades (from around $150 in 1991–93 to around $2000 today). By comparison, average adult full-time ordinary time earnings are slightly more than three times as large (from around $590 per week in 1991–93 to $1889 per week in 2023). Grange prices from Ray Byron and Orley Ashenfelter, 1995, 'Predicting the Quality of an Unborn Grange', *Economic Record*, Vol. 71, pp. 400–414 and Sterling Wine Auctions Grange prices (as at June 2024). Continuing on the culinary theme, one commentator posits a connection between inequality and excessive banquets: see Andrew Cornell, 2013, 'Devoured: Gourmet Gives Way to Glutton', *Australian Financial Review*, 2 February.

55 The share of people aged fourteen and over who used cocaine in the previous twelve months rose from 0.5 percent in 1993 to 4.2 percent in 2019: 1993 figure from Australian Institute of Health and Welfare, 2011, '2010 National Drug Strategy Household Survey: Detailed Findings', Drug Statistics Series, No. 25, Cat. No. PHE 145, AIHW, Canberra, p. 8; 2019 figure from Australian Institute of Health and Welfare, 2020, 'National Drug Strategy Household Survey 2019'. Drug Statistics Series, No. 32. PHE 270. Canberra AIHW, p. x.

56 Jacquie Hayes, 2012, 'First Class, Second Rate', *Australian Financial Review*, 11–12 August, p. 40.

57 Jacquie Hayes, 2012, 'Floored by Emirates', *Australian Financial Review*, 13–14 October, p. 40.

58 Jacquie Hayes, 2012, 'Luxury Beyond Cost', *Australian Financial Review*, 21–26 December 2012, p. 36; Rich Smith, 2024, '3 Things You Need to Know From Virgin Galactic's Earnings Call', *Motley Fool*, 16 March.

59 As an article in the *Australian Financial Review* magazine *Life and Leisure Luxury* puts it, 'Privacy is the new luxury': Lisa Carapiet, 2012, 'From the Discreet to the Bold, Luxury Charts New Territory', *Australian Financial Review Life and Leisure Luxury*, Autumn, pp. 32–39.

60 Jacquie Hayes, 2012, 'Get Piste, en Famille', *Australian Financial Review*, 2–4 January, p. 32.

61 Jacquie Hayes, 2012, 'A League of Their Own', *Australian Financial Review*, 1–2 September, p. 40.

62 On purchases of islands by the super-rich, see Melanie Beeby, Ben Wilmot and Matthew Cranston, 2012, 'Islands of the Rich and Famous', *BRW* magazine, 28 June.

63 Affordability data based on an analysis of 2022 HILDA data, using household weights. Child substantiations of maltreatment data from Australian Institute of Health and Welfare, 2024, *Child Protection Australia 2021–22*, CWS 92, AIHW, Canberra.

64 Hugh Mackay, 1995, *Society Now*, Mackay Research, Sydney, pp. 28–29.

65 Midnight Oil, 1982, 'Read About It' from the *10, 9, 8, 7, 6, 5, 4, 3, 2, 1* album.

Chapter 4

1 This is based on OECD figures for household disposable income in the most recent year: OECD, 2024, Income inequality (indicator). DOI: 10.1787/459aa7f1-en. The OECD is careful to ensure that its measures of inequality are comparable across countries. A similar picture emerges from data from the Luxembourg Income Study (lisdatacenter.org), whose figures are extremely comparable, but unfortunately only available for the early 2000s. Top incomes data are relatively comparable, and a similar picture emerges there too (see, for example, Leigh, 'How Closely Do Top Income Shares Track Other Measures of Inequality?' (see note 14, Chapter 1). Other datasets are much more problematic: for example, I avoid citing figures from the *World Income Inequality Database* (which is often used in World Bank and United Nations reports, but mixes income and consumption inequality). Work by Peter Whiteford suggests that wealth (as distinct from income) is more equally distributed in Australia than in several other countries, with one measure of wealth inequality placing us as the second-most equal of eleven advanced countries (see Peter Whiteford, 2012, 'Inequality and Redistribution in the Australian Welfare State' (see note 19, Chapter 3)).

2 Note that although globalisation has increased earnings inequality in Australia, it has also contributed to increasing living standards in China and India, which has reduced overall inequality across all world citizens. See, for example, Dollar and Kraay, 'Spreading the Wealth' (see note 32, Introduction); Milanovic, 'Global Income Inequality by the Numbers' (see note 32, Introduction).

3 Although the computer and internet revolutions represent a significant technological improvement, some economists argue that the pace of technological change was more rapid in the early part of the twentieth century, an era that saw breakthroughs in vehicles, aviation, sanitation, medicine, radio and telephones. See Tyler Cowen, 2011, *The Great Stagnation: How America Ate All the Low-Hanging Fruit of Modern History, Got Sick, and Will (Eventually) Feel Better*, Kindle edition, Dutton Adult. The issue is also discussed in 'Is the Ideas Machine Broken Down?', *The Economist*, 12 January 2013, pp. 19–22. For an Australian contribution, see Andrew Leigh, 2012, 'What Do We Eat after the Low-Hanging Fruit? A Brief Economic History of Australia, with Some Lessons for the Future', McKell Institute, Sydney, 18 May.

4 Sherwin Rosen, 1981, 'The Economics of Superstars', *American Economic Review*, Vol. 71, No. 5, pp. 845–58.

5 Billington's income is as quoted by Sherwin Rosen (see previous note). Pavarotti's income is from Michael Walsh, 1995, 'The Snake and the Fat Man', *New York Magazine*, 13 November. It is likely to be an underestimate of his peak career annual earnings.

6 Alan B. Krueger, 2019, *Rockonomics: A Backstage Tour of What the Music Industry Can Teach Us About Economics and Life*, Crown, New York.

7 Australian Bureau of Statistics, 2024, 'Are Taylor Swift tickets worth it?', https://twitter.com/ABSStats/status/1757902795372667036. The cheapest tickets to see Swift in 2024 were obstructed view seats, priced at $80.

8 Estimates for 1982–2012 were calculated for me by Jacob White, based on data for gross US audience revenue compiled at the website *Box Office Mojo* (boxofficemojo.com). With 400–600 films in the database, we opted to focus on the top 10 per cent share rather than the top 1 per cent share (which would only cover four to six films). I report 2022 for consistency with 1982, 1992 and so on (the 2023 figure was slightly lower, at 86 per cent). Another study that analyses this issue is Mark Weinstein, 1998, 'Profit-Sharing Contracts in Hollywood: Evolution and Analysis', *Journal of Legal Studies*, Vol. 27, No. 1, pp. 67–112. Weinstein estimates the revenue share of the top 1 per cent of films was 2–3 per cent in the late 1940s, 6 per cent in the early 1960s and 14 per cent in 1993. However, Weinstein's figures for the 1940s and 1960s strike me as implausibly low, and his 1993 estimate is based on only two out of 163 films, a smaller sample than is available at *Box Office Mojo*. Incidentally, the box office revenue share of *Spiderman: No Way Home* in 2021 would have been higher still had it not been released on 17 December.

9 Cited in Robert H. Frank and Philip J. Cook, 2010, *The Winner-Take-All Society: Why the Few at the Top Get So Much More than the Rest of Us*, Random House, New York, p. 194.

10 'The Highest-Paid Actors Of 2023', *Forbes*, 6 March 2024.

11 Michael Coelli and Jeff Borland, 2016, 'Job polarisation and earnings inequality in Australia', *Economic Record*, 92(296), pp. 1–27; Michael Coelli and Jeff Borland, 2019, 'Job polarisation and earnings inequality in Australia – an update', Report prepared for the Australian Government Department of Education, EDU19/2531, Department of Education, Canberra; Jeff Borland and Michael Coelli, 2023, 'The Australian labour market and IT-enabled technological change', Working paper, University of Melbourne.

12 David Nason, 2006, 'Bob Joss Now Bats for Other Team', *The Australian*, 9 October.

13 In the United States, there is some evidence that CEOs who receive prestigious business awards subsequently underperform their peers. Although they receive more compensation as a recognition of the award, they devote more time to activities such as media engagements and book-writing. As a result, these CEOs' firms do not perform as well as before winning the award. See Ulrike Malmendier and Geoffrey Tate, 2009, 'Superstar CEOs', *Quarterly Journal of Economics*, Vol. 124, No. 4, pp. 1593–1638.

14 This result comes from a 2009 Hewitt Csi survey that asked companies where they would position three elements of CEO pay: base pay, short-term incentives and long-term incentives. Precise answers differed across these elements, but the average was that about 45 per cent of firms would pay above median, about 50 per cent would pay the median, and about 5 per cent would pay below median. See David Peetz, 2010, 'Asymmetric Reference Points and the Growth of Executive Remuneration', Working Paper, Centre for Work, Organisation and Wellbeing, Griffith University, Brisbane.

15 Patrick Durkin and Les Hewitt, 2022, 'How much CEOs are really paid (in 7 charts)' *Australian Financial Review*, 20 July; 'CEO pay continues to soar – new study', *Human Resources Director*, 8 May 2023.

16 Leigh, How Closely Do Top Income Shares Track Other Measures of Inequality?' (see note 14, Chapter 1).

17 Emmanuel Saez and Michael Veall, 2005, 'The Evolution of High Incomes in Northern America: Lessons from Canadian Evidence', *American Economic Review*, Vol. 95, No. 3, pp. 831–49.

18 This is reflected in the Australian Council of Trade Unions' historical pattern of pushing for flat-dollar increases in federal wage cases. Joshua Healy, 2011, 'The Quest for Fairness in Australian Minimum Wages', *Journal of Industrial Relations*, Vol. 53, No. 5, pp. 662–680. In the 2017 federal minimum wage case, the ACTU called for a 6.7 per cent increase for the lowest paid workers, and a 5.7 per cent increase for higher-paid award workers: ACTU, 2017, *ACTU Submission to the Annual Wage Review 2016–17*, ACTU, Melbourne. More recently, the ACTU has tended to advocate for a common percentage increase across all award minimum wages.

19 For example, the ACTU has proposed capping CEO salaries at ten times average earnings, limiting tax-deductibility on executive salaries over $1 million, and allowing shareholders to sue underperforming executives: ACTU, 2012, 'Executive Pay Watch', ACTU, Melbourne.

20 Reg Hamilton (ed.), 2011, *Waltzing Matilda and the Sunshine Harvester Factory: The Early History of the Arbitration Court, the Australian Minimum Wage, Working Hours and Paid Leave*, Fair Work Australia, Melbourne, pp. 147, 162.

21 Union membership rates from 1976 to 2022 are published as Australian Bureau of Statistics, 2022, *Trade Union Membership*, ABS, Canberra, 14 September. These are derived from employee surveys – generally regarded as the most accurate source (drawn from ABS 6323.0, 6325.0, 6310.0, 6333.0, 6335.0). For earlier years, we only have estimates from union surveys (drawn from David Peetz, 1998, *Unions in a Contrary World: The Future of the Australian Trade Union Movement*, Cambridge University Press, Melbourne, p. 26). Union survey estimates are invariably higher, since they include people who belong to multiple unions, and those who are no longer financial members. In 1976, the estimate in the employee surveys was 7.8 per cent lower than the estimate in the union surveys. To make the two series comparable, I therefore scaled down the union survey number for 1911–1975 by 7.8 per cent. For 1891–1910, I drew on trade union membership figures and labour force figures from the Census Bureau, compiled in Glenn Withers, Tony Endres and Len Perry, 1985, 'Australian Historical Statistics: Labour Statistics', Source Papers in Economic History, ANU, Canberra. These Census Bureau figures are scaled up to match the adjusted Peetz series by 50.3 per cent, being the ratio of the two overlap years (1911 and 1912).

22 In the United States, John DiNardo, Nicole M. Fortin and Thomas Lemieux found that changes in unionisation rates and the level of the real minimum wage accounted for a substantial proportion of the rise in US inequality from 1979–88. See John DiNardo, Nicole M. Fortin and Thomas Lemieux, 1996, 'Labor Market Institutions and the Distribution of Wages, 1973–1992: A Semiparametric Approach', *Econometrica*, Vol. 64, No. 5, pp. 1001–44. In cross-country analysis, David Card, Thomas Lemieux, and W. Craig Riddell

analysed Canada, the United Kingdom and the United States, and concluded that in all three countries, differences in unionisation rates have a strong impact on inequality, especially among males. Their study also suggests that differences in unionisation rates explain up to two-thirds of the inequality gap between the United Kingdom and United States. See David Card, Thomas Lemieux and W. Craig Riddell, 2003, 'Unionization and Wage Inequality: A Comparative Study of the US, the UK, and Canada', NBER Working Paper 9473, NBER, Cambridge, MA. Related economic evidence suggests that unions are responsible for significant improvements in workplace safety: see Alejandro Donado and Klaus Wälde, 2012, 'How Trade Unions Increase Welfare', *Economic Journal*, Vol. 122, pp. 990–1009.

23 Jeff Borland found that changes in union density could explain approximately 30 per cent of the increase in variance of male full-time earnings between 1986 and 1994, and around 15 per cent of the increase in variance of female earnings. See Jeff Borland, 1995, 'Union Effects on Earnings Dispersion in Australia, 1986–94', *British Journal of Industrial Relations*, Vol. 34, No. 2, pp. 237–248. See also Ann Harding, 1997, 'The Suffering Middle: Trends in Income Inequality in Australia, 1982 to 1993–94', Discussion Paper No. 21, NATSEM, Canberra; Jeff Borland and Roger Wilkins, 1996, 'Earnings Inequality in Australia', *Economic Record*, Vol. 72, No. 216, pp. 7–23.

24 From 1983 to 2023, the US unionisation rate fell from 20.1 to 10.0 per cent, suggesting that union membership rates are now much more similar in the two countries than they were in the 1980s.

25 B.K. de Garis, 1974, '1890–1900', in *A New History of Australia* (see note 19, Chapter 2), pp. 216–259. Similarly, high inequality in early twentieth century America helped motivate that country's reintroduction of a federal income tax in 1913: Jill Lepore, 2012, 'Tax Time', *The New Yorker*, 26 November, pp. 24–29.

26 Total Australian taxation for 1850 to 1968 is set out in Alan Barnard, 1987, 'Government Finance', in *Australians: Historical Statistics* (see note 28, Chapter 1), pp. 282–83.

27 William Bateman, 1904, *Present Taxation and Its Inequality*, Chronicle General Printing Office, Melbourne, pp. 3–4.

28 For the period when states levied income taxes, I assumed that the taxpayer lived in the largest jurisdiction (NSW). When taxes differed on wage and investment income, I assumed that the income was wage income. The rate graphed is the marginal rate, with the lower estimate being the marginal tax rate that applied on income at the 99.5th percentile (that is, the median marginal tax rate of the top 1 per cent). Sincere gratitude to my research assistants Elena Varganova and Susanne Schmidt, each of whom spent about a month interpreting Australia's state and federal tax laws in the early twentieth century.

29 In 2007, both major parties went to the election with an 'aspirational' promise to reduce the top rate to 40 per cent. Since then, however, most of the focus has been around adjusting lower rates, and the threshold from which the top tax rate applies.

30 A small Australian capital gains tax existed back as far as at least the late 1960s: see Richard Burkhauser, Markus Hahn and Roger Wilkins, 2013, 'Recent Trends in Top Incomes Share in Australia: Why Separating Capitals Gains in Tax Record Data Matters', Paper Presented at the ASSA Meetings, January 2013. Roger Wilkins informs me that it typically raised around 0.03 per cent of taxable income in the 1970s.

31 This change also shifted the capital gains tax base from real capital gains to nominal capital gains, but only a minority of capital gains taxpayers were adversely affected by the switch.

32 Anthony B. Atkinson and Andrew Leigh, 2013, 'The Distribution of Top Incomes in Five Anglo-Saxon Countries over the Long Run', *Economic Record*, Vol. 89, Issue S1, pp. 31–47.

33 Claudia Goldin and Larry Katz, 2008, *The Race between Education and Technology*, Harvard University Press, Cambridge, MA.

34 In 1901, the literacy rate across the over-five population was 93 per cent. Prior literacy estimates are based on the share of brides and grooms who signed the marriage register, which averaged 75 per cent in 1861, 86 per cent in 1871 and 99 per cent in 1901. See Alison Booth and Hiau Kee, 2011, 'A Long-Run View of the University Gender Gap in Australia', *Australian Economic History Review*, Vol. 51, No. 3, pp. 254–76.

35 Australian Bureau of Statistics, 2023, 'Education and Work, Australia, May 2023', ABS, Canberra, Table 35; Australia Bureau of Statistics, 2024, 'Schools: Data on government and non-government students, staff and schools', ABS, Canberra, Graph 5; Lyn Robinson and Stephen Lamb, 2012, *How Young People Are Faring 2012*, Foundation for Young Australians, Melbourne.

36 Compared with other OECD nations, Australia ranks better on university attainment than we do on attainment of Year 12 or its equivalent: see Robinson and Lamb, *How Young People Are Faring 2012* (see note 35, Chapter 4), pp. 60 and 62 (Figs 39 and 41).

37 Average years of education are estimated by Christian Morrisson and Fabrice Murtin, 2009, 'The Century of Education', *Journal of Human Capital*, Vol. 3, No. 1, pp. 1–42. For the working-age population (aged 15–64), Morrisson and Murtin estimate that the average number of years of education in each decade was 2.12 (1870), 3.47 (1880), 5.51 (1890), 6.59 (1900), 7.41 (1910), 8.00 (1920), 8.69 (1930), 8.83 (1940), 8.96 (1950), 9.24 (1960), 11.04 (1970), 12.20 (1980), 12.76 (1990), 13.09 (2000) and 13.25 (2010).

38 Indeed, Australian educational attainment fell in the 1930s. As one study notes, 'when fees were increased, extended or reintroduced, as in almost all States during the Depression, secondary school enrolments fell markedly': G. Burke and A. Spaull, 2001, 'Education and Training. Centenary Article – Australian Schools: Participation and Funding 1901–2000', in Australian Bureau of Statistics, *Year Book 2001*, ABS, Canberra. A picture of Australian schooling in 1960 can be had from the quote attributed to one Victorian schoolboy in that year: 'They're getting real tough – they're even taking our tobacco away from us now': *Australians: Historical Statistics* (see note 28, Chapter 1), p. 338.

39 A similar picture emerges from looking at the share of people employed in the Education, Museums and Libraries sector (which is dominated by schoolteachers, vocational educators and university lecturers). From 1901 to 1961, this figure rose from 2.1 to 3.2 per cent. But by 1981, it had risen to 6.7 per cent. See Michael Carter, 1987, 'The Service Sector', in Rodney Maddock and Ian W. McLean (eds), *The Australian Economy in the Long Run*, Cambridge University Press, Cambridge, pp. 195–226, Table 8.5.

40 These estimates are from Andrew Leigh, 2024, 'Returns to Education in Australia 2001–2022', *Economic Papers*, forthcoming. Survey respondents with zero earnings are assumed not to have a job.

41 The percentage effects are from ibid. The dollar estimate is from Andrew Norton, 2013, *Mapping Australian Higher Education*, 2013 version, Grattan Institute, Melbourne, p. 71. There is also good evidence that education pays off in non-economic ways, such as through better health, more happiness, less crime, and more civic activity. See for example Philip Oreopoulos, 2007, 'Do Dropouts Drop Out Too Soon? Wealth, Health and Happiness from Compulsory Schooling', *Journal of Public Economics*, Vol. 91, Nos 11–12, pp. 2213–29.

42 Leigh, 'Returns to Education in Australia 2001–2022' (see note 40, Chapter 4); Mick Coelli and Roger Wilkins, 2009, 'Credential Changes and Education Earnings Premia in Australia', *Economic Record*, Vol. 85, No. 270, pp. 239–59.

43 Andrew Leigh and Chris Ryan, 2011, 'Long-Run Trends in School Productivity: Evidence from Australia', *Education Finance and Policy*, Vol. 6, No. 1, pp. 105–135.

44 OECD, 2023, *PISA 2022 Results: Factsheets, Australia*, OECD, Paris, 5 December.

45 Australian Curriculum, Assessment and Reporting Authority, 2023, *NAPLAN National Results 2008–2022* [Archive], ACARA, Sydney. Results from 2023 onwards are not comparable with earlier years.

46 Australian students improved on year 4 mathematics and science and year 8 science, but not on year 8 mathematics: Sue Thomson, Nicole Wernert, Sima Rodrigues and Elizabeth O'Grady, 2020, *TIMSS 2019 Australia, Highlights*, Australian Council for Educational Research, Melbourne, p. 12.

47 These data are drawn from Stephen Nickell, 2004, 'Poverty and Worklessness in Britain', *Economic Journal*, Vol. 114, No. 494, pp. C1–C25. Nickell assumes that Ireland has the same level of test score inequality as the United Kingdom. See also Eric A. Hanushek and Ludger Woessmann, 2011, 'The Economics of International Differences in Educational Achievement', in Eric A. Hanushek, Stephen Machin and Ludger Woessmann (eds), *Handbook of the Economics of Education*, Volume 3, North Holland, Amsterdam, pp. 89–200. I have been unable to find published 90/10 ratios for more recent international tests, but a similar exercise using different inequality measures (for example, comparing OECD Gini coefficients for the late 2000s with the 95–5 difference in 2009 PISA scores, with the sample restricted to countries whose GDP exceeds US$25,000) produces similar results. I am grateful to Gus Little for

tabulating these data. Socioeconomic attainment gaps among Year 3 students from Lisa O'Brien, 2023, *Improving Outcomes for All: The Report of the Independent Expert Panel's Review to Inform a Better and Fairer Education System*, Department of Education, Canberra, p. 33.

48 For example, an increase in assortative mating (in which people tend to marry those of a similar socioeconomic bracket) had a relatively small impact on household inequality over this period: Jared Greenville, Clinton Pobke and Nikki Rogers, 2013, *Trends in the Distribution of Income in Australia*, Productivity Commission Staff Working Paper, Canberra, p. 133.

49 For example, see Australian Government, 1995, *Enterprising Nation: Renewing Australia's Managers to Meet the Challenges of the Asia-Pacific Century*, Department of Employment, Education and Training, Canberra.

Chapter 5

1 From 1888–89 to 2022–23, the English Premier League and its predecessor tournaments completed 124 seasons (with 11 cancelled due to World Wars I and II). From 1897 to 2023, the AFL, and before that the VFL, completed 127 seasons (with no war cancellations).

2 James Ducker, 2023, 'Man City smash Man Utd's finance record despite £400m salary bill', *The Telegraph*, 15 November.

3 Geelong's submission correctly points out that what matters for competitive balance isn't the total amount of funding; it's the distribution of that funding. They point out that average club revenue was $300,000 in 1975, $3 million in 1985, and $42 million in 2013, but they argue that the inequality of funding has grown over this period: Colin Carter and Brian Cook, 2013, 'Geelong Cats Response to AFL on Equalisation', February 2013. Similarly, an article by Michael Warner points out that 'No team in the bottom four of football department spending has won a premiership since North Melbourne in 1999.': Michael Warner, 2013, 'Stars Pan Rich Club, Poor Club System and Claim Chasm Is Widening', *The Herald Sun*, 18 March.

4 From 1888–89 to 1969–70, Arsenal, Everton, Liverpool and Manchester United each won 7 championships, equating to 9.9 per cent apiece of the seventy-one championships held in this era. In the AFL, Collingwood won thirteen of the seventy-four premierships held in this era (17.6 per cent).

5 From 1993–94 to 2022–23, Chelsea won five championships (16.7 per cent), Manchester City won seven championships (23.3 per cent) and Manchester United won twelve championships (40.0 per cent).

6 For more detail, see Andrew Leigh, 2018, 'The Postcode Paradox: Why is Australian Intergenerational Mobility So Low, and What Can we Do to Increase It?' Evatt Foundation NSW Parliament Lecture, Sydney, 25 September.

7 Robert Breunig et al., 2012, 'Wage Dispersion and Team Performance: A Theoretical Model and Evidence from Baseball', ANU CEPR Discussion Paper 663, ANU, Canberra.

8 Both Lucas and Feldstein are quoted in Branko Milanovic, 2007, 'Why We All Care About Inequality (But Some of Us Are Loathe to Admit It)', *Challenge*, Vol. 50, No. 6, pp. 109–120.

9 J.B. Davies et al., 2008, 'The World Distribution of Household Wealth', in J.B. Davies (ed.), *Personal Wealth from a Global Perspective*, Oxford University Press, Oxford, pp. 395–418.

10 Matthew Thomas, 2012, 'Homelessness in Australia – Official ABS Estimates', *FlagPost*, September 13 (parliamentflagpost.blogspot.com.au/2012/09/homelessness-in-australia-official-abs.html).

11 This is also true of other comparisons across society. For example, one scholar notes that a speedy car in 1950 would be regarded as sluggish today, that what constitutes a large house depends on the neighbourhood, and that whether someone is wearing a good suit to their job interview depends on the garb of the other job applicants: Robert Frank, 2007, *Falling Behind: How Rising Inequality Harms the Middle Class,* University of California Press, Berkeley, CA.

12 Richard Tawney, 1913, 'Poverty as an Industrial Problem', Inaugural Lecture, reproduced in *Memoranda on the Problems of Poverty*, William Morris Press, London.

13 Adam Smith, 1759, *The Theory of Moral Sentiments*, A. Millar, A. Kincaid and J. Bell, London, Chapter 3.

14 Sandy Baum, 1992, 'Poverty, Inequality and the Role of Government: What Would Adam Smith Say?', *Eastern Economic Journal*, Vol. 18, No. 2, pp. 143–156.

15 See, for example, Simon Kuznets, 1955, 'Economic Growth and Income Inequality', *American Economic Review*, Vol. 45, No. 1, pp. 1–28; Amartya Sen, 2009, *The Idea of Justice*, Harvard University Press & Allen Lane, Cambridge, MA; Joseph Stiglitz, 2013, *The Price of Inequality: How Today's Divided Society Endangers Our Future*, W.W. Norton & Company, New York; Paul Krugman, 2007, *The Conscience of a Liberal*, W.W. Norton & Company, New York.

16 Dan Andrews, Christopher Jencks and Andrew Leigh, 2011, 'Do Rising Top Incomes Lift All Boats?' *B.E. Journal of Economic Analysis & Policy* (Contributions), Vol. 11, No. 1, Article 6.

17 For example, Australian entrepreneurs often complain about the paucity of funds available from 'the FFF fund': friends, family and fools (see, for example, Bina Brown, 2012, 'Angels, Incubators Lend Ventures a Hand, *Australian Financial Review*, 14–15 July). One potential benefit of higher top incomes is that they might increase the amount of money available for entrepreneurs from informal sources. My own research found the impact of inequality on savings to be small or non-existent (Andrew Leigh and Alberto Posso, 2009, 'Top Incomes and National Savings', *Review of Income and Wealth*, Vol. 55, No. 1, pp. 57–74), but this does not rule out a targeted investment channel.

18 Martin Gilens, 2005, 'Inequality and Democratic Responsiveness', *Public Opinion Quarterly*, Vol. 69, No. 5, pp. 778–796; Larry Bartels, 2008, *Unequal Democracy: The Political Economy of the New Gilded Age*, Russell Sage Foundation and Princeton University Press, New York. See also an intriguing analysis of the political preferences of wealthiest 1 per cent: Benjamin I. Page, Larry M. Bartels and Jason Seawright, 2011, 'Democracy

and the Policy Preferences of Wealthy Americans', Paper presented at the American Political Science Association, Seattle, WA.

19 Plato, 1955, *The Republic*, translated by Desmond Lee, Penguin, New York. Aristotle took the view that in an unequal democracy the redistributive attempts of the poor would be countered by the elitist attempts of the rich. For a discussion of this issue, see John Ferejohn and Frances Rosenbluth, 2006, 'Toward a Republican Liberalism', SSRN Working Paper 1154097.

20 Mark Aguiar and Erik Hurst, 2008, 'The Increase in Leisure Inequality', NBER Working Paper No. 13837, NBER, Cambridge, MA.

21 John Rawls, 1971, *The Theory of Justice*, Harvard University Press, Cambridge, MA. There have been several critiques of Rawls over the ensuing four decades. For example, Amartya Sen argues that it is far from obvious that people behind the veil would make the distributional decisions Rawls posits. For example, Sen uses the example of three children making claims to a flute, and contends that children might reasonably argue for it because they are the most talented player (a utilitarian argument), because they made the flute (an effort-based argument), or because they are the poorest (an egalitarian argument). Behind the veil, Sen says, all three principles could reasonably be supported. See Sen, *The Idea of Justice* (see note 15, Chapter 5). Others have also noted that the veil should be extended to ignorance over one's country of birth, an extension with important implications for global justice. See, for example, Thomas Pogge, 1989, *Realizing Rawls*, Cornell University Press, Ithaca; Peter Singer, 2002, *One World: The Ethics of Globalization*, Yale University Press, New Haven, CT.

22 This paragraph draws on arguments made by Harvard philosopher Michael Sandel in his undergraduate course on 'Justice'.

23 Lester C. Thurow, 1971, 'The Income Distribution as a Pure Public Good', *Quarterly Journal of Economics*, Vol. 85, No. 2, pp. 327–336.

24 Lateral Economics, 2011, *The Herald/Age – Lateral Economics Index of Australia's Wellbeing, Final Report*, Lateral Economics, Melbourne, p. 43. As the report acknowledges, interpersonal utility comparisons have a controversial history within economics, with some instead preferring the more conservative but less tractable Pareto approach (we can only be certain of an increase in wellbeing if no one is worse off and someone is better off). Note too that Rawls' approach is explicitly not a utilitarian one, since he believes that income differences are only justifiable if they raise the wellbeing of the most disadvantaged.

25 Sara Solnick and David Hemenway, 1998, 'Is More Always Better?: A Survey on Positional Concerns', *Journal of Economic Behavior and Organization*, Vol. 37, No. 3, pp. 373–383. Positional concerns were least important (relative to absolute concerns) when the subject was the number of weeks' holiday per year.

26 For reviews of the ultimatum game literature, see, for example, Hessel Oosterbeek, Randolph Sloof and Gijs van de Kuilen, 2004, 'Cultural Differences in Ultimatum Game Experiments: Evidence from a Meta-Analysis', *Experimental Economics*, Vol. 7, No. 2, pp. 171–188; Joseph

Bearden, 2001, 'Ultimatum Bargaining Experiments: The State of the Art', available at SSRN (ssrn.com/abstract=626183).

27 Christopher T. Dawes et al., 2007, 'Egalitarian Motives in Humans', *Nature*, Vol. 446, pp. 794–796.

28 Other economics games that find behaviour consistent with a desire to reduce inequality are public good games with punishment, prisoner's dilemma games, trust games, the moonlighting game and the gift exchange game.

29 See, for example, Jimmy A. Frazier and Eldon E. Snyder, 1991, 'The Underdog Concept in Sport', *Sociology of Sport Journal*, Vol. 8, No. 4, pp. 380–388; Nadav Goldschmied and Joseph A. Vandello, 2009, 'The Advantage of Disadvantage: Underdogs in the Political Arena', *Basic and Applied Social Psychology*, Vol. 31, No. 1, pp. 24–31; Nadav P. Goldschmied and Joseph A. Vandello. 2012, 'The Future Is Bright: The Underdog Label, Availability, and Optimism', *Basic and Applied Social Psychology*, Vol. 34, No. 1, pp. 34–43.

30 Quoted in Steven D. Levitt and Stephen J. Dubner, 2009, *Superfreakonomics: Global Cooling, Patriotic Prostitutes and Why Suicide Bombers Should Buy Life Insurance*, William Morrow, New York.

31 Erzo Luttmer, 2005, 'Neighbors as Negatives: Relative Earnings and Well-Being', *Quarterly Journal of Economics*, Vol. 120, No. 3, pp. 963–1002. The effect is so large that a $100 increase in an individual's own income has the same effect on happiness as a $100 decrease in their neighbours' incomes (where neighbourhoods are defined as Public Use Microdata Areas, each containing around 150,000 people).

32 David Card et al., 2012, 'Inequality at Work: The Effect of Peer Salaries on Job Satisfaction', *American Economic Review*, Vol. 102, No. 6, pp. 2981–3003. The institution is the University of California, and results are compared against a randomly selected control group that was not encouraged to check their co-workers' earnings.

33 Alberto Alesina, Rafael Di Tella and Robert MacCulloch, 2004, 'Inequality and Happiness: Are Europeans and Americans Different?', *Journal of Public Economics*, Vol. 88, Nos 9–10, pp. 2009–2042.

34 For example, another study looks at employees who work in pairs, and finds clear evidence that earnings relativities matter. Specifically, the impact of a wage cut on productivity is much larger if the person's co-worker does not suffer the same wage cut: Alain Cohn et al., 2011, 'Social Comparison in the Workplace: Evidence from a Field Experiment', IZA DP 5550, IZA, Bonn.

35 Quoted in Luttmer, 'Neighbors as Negatives: Relative Earnings and Well-Being' (see note 31, Chapter 5), pp. 963–1002.

36 See Frank, *Falling Behind* (see note 11, Chapter 5).

37 Statistic from Bruce Tranter and Dallas Hanson, 2010, 'Surfing the Scalpel: Cosmetic Surgery, Attraction and Body Image in Australia', TASA 2010 Conference Proceedings: Social Causes, Private Lives, 6–9 December 2010, Sydney. See also Meredith Jones, 2008, *Skintight: An Anatomy of Cosmetic Surgery*, Berg, New York. Statistics on the prevalence of plastic surgery are difficult to come by, but it is noteworthy that the number of private

hospitals offering cosmetic surgery in Australia increased by 14 per cent from 2006–07 to 2008–09: ABS, 2010, *Private Hospitals, Australia, 2008–09*. Cat. No. 4390.0, ABS, Canberra.

38 The story of the rise and fall of Venice is set out in Daron Acemoglu and James A. Robinson, 2012, *Why Nations Fail: The Origins of Power, Prosperity, and Poverty*, Crown, New York. I have also drawn on the account of their work by Chrystia Freeland, 2012, 'The Self-Destruction of the 1 per cent', *The New York Times*, 13 October.

39 Cited in Hugh Dalton, 1925, *Some Aspects of the Inequality of Incomes in Modern Communities*, Routledge, London, p. 21.

40 Richard G. Wilkinson and Kate Pickett, 2009, *The Spirit Level: Why More Equal Societies Almost Always Do Better*, Allen Lane, London, p. 261.

41 For specific analyses of the difference between looking at inequality and health using cross-sectional rather than panel data, see Andrew Leigh, Christopher Jencks and Tim Smeeding, 2009, 'Health and Inequality', in Wiemer Salverda, Brian Nolan and Timothy M. Smeeding (eds), *The Oxford Handbook of Economic Inequality*, Oxford University Press, Oxford, pp. 384–405. More generally, Wilkinson and Pickett have been criticised by a number of reviewers. See for example John Kay, 2009, 'The Spirit Level', *Financial Times*, 23 March; Tim Harford, 2010, 'More or Less', *BBC Radio 4*, 27 April; Scott Winship, 2013, 'Overstating the Costs of Inequality', *National Affairs*, No. 15.

42 The 'thumb test' for outliers is suggested by Christian Bjørnskov, 2009, 'The Spirit Level: Why Greater Equality Makes Societies Stronger', *Population and Development Review*, Vol. 36, No. 2, pp. 395–397.

43 My own findings are set out in Andrew Leigh and Christopher Jencks, 2007, 'Inequality and Mortality: Long-Run Evidence from a Panel of Countries', *Journal of Health Economics*, Vol. 26, No. 1, pp. 1–24; Leigh, Jencks and Smeeding, 'Health and Inequality' (see note 41, Chapter 5), pp. 384–405. Other useful reviews of this literature include Angus Deaton, 2003, 'Health, Inequality, and Economic Development', *Journal of Economic Literature*, Vol. 41, pp. 113–158; J. Lynch et al., 2004, 'Is Income Inequality a Determinant of Population Health? Part 1: A Systematic Review', *Milbank Quarterly*, Vol. 82. No. 1, pp. 5–99; K. Judge, J. Mulligan and M. Benzeval, 1998, 'Income Inequality and Population Health', *Social Science and Medicine*, Vol. 46, Nos 4–5, pp. 567–79.

44 Samantha Bricknell, 2023, *Homicide in Australia 2020–21*, Australian Institute of Criminology, Canberra; Katharina Buchholz, 2023, 'U.S. Homicide Rate Comes Down From Pandemic Peak', *Statistica*, 18 October. I focus on homicide because it is the best-measured crime category. See also Leigh, Jencks and Smeeding, 'Health and Inequality' (see note 41, Chapter 5).

Chapter 6

1 Rubinstein, *The All-Time Australian 200 Rich List* (see note 20, Chapter 1).

2 McGregor, *Profile of Australia* (see note 37, Chapter 2), p. 110.

3 Donald Horne, 1964, *The Lucky Country: Australia in the Sixties*, Penguin, Ringwood, Vic.

4 Andrew Leigh, 2007, 'Intergenerational Mobility in Australia', *The B.E. Journal of Economic Analysis & Policy*, Vol. 7, No. 2 (Contributions), Article 6. Both fathers' and sons' earnings are measured when they are aged around forty (the age at which current earnings are the best proxy for lifetime earnings). .

5 This example is drawn from Alan B. Krueger, 2012, 'The Rise and Consequences of Inequality in the United States', Speech at the Center for American Progress, 12 January. A study looking at the correlation in siblings' outcomes finds a higher correlation in incomes than height or weight (Bhashkar Mazumder, 2008, 'Sibling Similarities and Economic Inequality in the US', *Journal of Population Economics*, Vol. 21, No. 3, pp. 685–701), a result that prompted one commentator to conclude 'I am less the master of my fate than I am of my body mass index': Timothy Noah, 2012, *The Great Divergence: America's Growing Inequality Crisis and What We Can Do About It*, Bloomsbury Press, New York.

6 Silvia Mendolia and Peter Siminski, 2016, 'New estimates of intergenerational mobility in Australia', *Economic Record*, vol. 92, no. 298, pp. 361–373; Chelsea Murray, Robert Graham Clark, Silvia Mendolia and Peter Siminski, 2018, 'Direct measures of intergenerational income mobility for Australia', *Economic Record*, vol. 94, no. 307, pp. 445–468; Nathan Deutscher and Bhashkar Mazumder, 2020, 'Intergenerational mobility across Australia and the stability of regional estimates', *Labour Economics*, vol. 66, article 101861; Peter Siminski and Sin Hung Yu, 2022, 'The correlation of wealth between parents and children in Australia', *Australian Economic Review*, vol. 55, no. 2, pp. 195–214. For a longer run perspective, see Gregory Clark, Andrew Leigh and Mike Pottenger, 2020, 'Frontiers of mobility: Was Australia 1870–2017 a more socially mobile society than England?' *Explorations in Economic History*, vol. 76, article 101327.

7 Nathan Deutscher and Bhashkar Mazumder, 2020, 'Intergenerational mobility across Australia and the stability of regional estimates', *Labour Economics*, vol. 66, article 101861; Silvia Mendolia and Peter Siminski, 2017, 'Is education the mechanism through which family background affects economic outcomes? A generalised approach to mediation analysis', *Economics of Education Review*, vol. 59, pp. 1–12; Chelsea Murray, Robert Graham Clark, Silvia Mendolia and Peter Siminski, 2018, 'Direct measures of intergenerational income mobility for Australia', *Economic Record*, vol. 94, no. 307, pp. 445–468.

8 Tomas Kennedy and Peter Siminski, 2022, 'Are We Richer Than Our Parents Were? Absolute Income Mobility in Australia', *Economic Record*, vol. 98, pp. 22–41.

9 Christopher Jencks and Laura Tach, 2006, 'Would Equal Opportunity Mean More Mobility?', in S. Morgan, D. Grusky and G. Fields (eds), *Mobility and Inequality: Frontiers of Research from Sociology and Economics*, Stanford University Press, Stanford.

10 Dan Andrews and Andrew Leigh, 2009, 'More Inequality, Less Social Mobility', *Applied Economics Letters*, Vol. 16, pp. 1489–1492.

11 Krueger, 'The Rise and Consequences of Inequality in the United States' (see note 5, Chapter 6).
12 Miles Corak, 2013, 'Inequality from Generation to Generation: The United States in Comparison', in Robert Rycroft (ed.), *The Economics of Inequality, Poverty, and Discrimination in the Twenty-first Century*, ABC-CLIO, Santa Barbara, CA. Note that we cannot yet shed light on the issue using purely Australian data (see next note).
13 My own study compared social mobility across multiple cohorts, and found that father–son mobility was no different for sons born in 1911–1940 than for sons born in 1949–1979. Because the latter cohort mostly grew up after the recent rise in inequality, it is unlikely that I would have been able to detect the impact of the post-1980 rise in inequality on Australian social mobility. See Leigh, 'Intergenerational Mobility in Australia' (see note 4, Chapter 6)
14 This analysis uses the 2022 HILDA survey, and is based on financial and non-financial inheritances.
15 Intergenerational mobility appears to have fallen in the United States (Daniel Aaronson and Bhashkar Mazumder, 2008, 'Intergenerational Economic Mobility in the US: 1940 to 2000', *Journal of Human Resources*, Vol. 43, No. 1, pp. 139–172), and in the United Kingdom (J. Blanden et al., 2004, 'Changes in Intergenerational Mobility in Britain', in M. Corak (ed.), *Generational Income Mobility in North America and Europe*, Cambridge University Press, Cambridge, pp. 122–146). For Australia, my research found little change from the 1960s to the 2000s. Because I am using lower-quality data than the US and UK researchers, one possibility is that it is simply harder to detect the change in Australia. The other possibility is that social mobility stayed fairly constant over that period. This could be because the forces that might have reduced social mobility (rising income inequality, changing family structure, the abolition of inheritance taxes) were offset by forces that worked to increase social mobility (more education places, universal health care, the banning of racial discrimination).
16 Barack Obama, Address to the Democratic Convention, 27 July 2004.
17 Barack Obama, 2013, 'Remarks by the President on Economic Mobility', Washington DC, 4 December. See also Hayes, *Twilight of the Elites* (see note 54, Chapter 2).
18 Daniel P. Moynihan, 1965, 'The Negro Family: The Case for National Action', Office of Planning and Research, United States Department of Labor.
19 To me, the sale of slave children sums up better than any other statistic the inhumanity of that system. Source: David Blight, 2008, 'HIST 119: The Civil War and Reconstruction Era, 1845–1877', Yale University, New Haven, CT, Lecture 3 (podcast available at oyc.yale.edu/history/hist-119).
20 William Ryan, 1976, *Blaming the Victim*, Vintage, New York.
21 Current figure is from the 2021 census, as reported in Australian Institute of Family Studies, 2023, 'Families and family composition', AIFS, Canberra. The 1970s estimates are from David de Vaus, 2004, *Diversity and Change in Australian Families: Statistical Profiles*, Australian Institute of Family Studies, Melbourne, p. 43.

22 Alan Hayes et al., 2010, 'Families Then and Now: 1980–2010', Australian Institute of Family Studies, Melbourne.
23 PHIDU, 2023, 'Aboriginal single parent families with children aged less than 15 years, 2021', Torrens University, Adelaide.
24 The analysis was conducted using the family history questions in the HILDA survey. To maximise sample size, I use respondents in all waves from 2005 (when parental education questions were first asked) to 2022. University education includes parents whose highest post-school qualification is from a teacher's college or a college of advanced education (which became universities in the 1990s). Analysis excludes people where only one parent had a university degree. All analysis uses household weights. Results in Figure 13 are five-year averages. Unfortunately, the way these questions are constructed in the HILDA survey does not allow me to include the children of same-sex couples. A similar pattern emerges if I use just mothers' education or fathers' education.
25 Genevieve Heard finds a similar trend in census statistics, though her unit of analysis is partnerships rather than children. For example, among people in their early forties, 16 per cent of university-educated men were not in a partnership in 2006, compared with 32 per cent among men without qualifications. A similar story emerges for women. From 1996 to 2006, Heard finds a divergence across educational lines. University graduates are just as likely to partner up as they were in the 1990s, but partnering rates have fallen for the least educated. See Genevieve Heard, 2008, 'Partnerships at the 2006 Census: Preliminary Findings', *People and Place*, Vol. 16, No. 1, pp. 31–39.
26 For example, fifteen-year-old children in lone-parent families score on average twenty-seven points less on the PISA maths test (equivalent to about half a year of learning). See Anna D'Addio, 2008, 'Intergenerational Mobility: Does It Offset or Reinforce Income Inequality?', in OECD, *Growing Unequal?* OECD, Paris, p. 211. Other research shows that young children in sole-parent families have worse outcomes in terms of hyperactivity, physical development, and social-emotional development: Lixia Qu and Ruth Weston, 2012, 'Parental Marital Status and Children's Wellbeing', Department of Families, Housing, Community Services and Indigenous Affairs Occasional Paper No. 46, FaHCSIA, Canberra, pp. 24–25.
27 ABS, 1994, *Births Australia 1993* (Cat. No. 3301.0), ABS, Canberra; ABS, 2023, *Births Australia 2022*, ABS, Canberra. Over the period since 1971, the biggest increase seems to have taken place in the 1980s. The share of births to unmarried couples was 9 per cent in 1971, 13 per cent in 1981, 23 per cent in 1991, 31 per cent in 2001, 34 per cent in 2010, and 40 per cent in 2022.
28 McGregor, *Profile of Australia* (see note 37, Chapter 2), p. 67.
29 Latest figures from ABS, *Births Australia 2022* (see note 27, Chapter 6). 1990s statistics on nuptiality of First Nations births are not available for all jurisdictions, but the ABS data show that in South Australia, the share of First Nations births to unmarried parents rose from 76 per cent in 1991 to 84 per cent in 2001 and in the Northern Territory from 92 per cent in 1991

to 95 per cent in 2001. There has been little change since then. Across Australia, the share of First Nations births to unmarried parents was 81 per cent in 2001 and 82 per cent in 2022.

30 ABS, *Births Australia 2022* (see note 27, Chapter 6).

31 Laura Tach, Kathy Edin and Sara McLanahan, 'Multiple Partners and Multiple Partner Fertility in Fragile Families, Fragile Families Working Paper WP11-10-FF.

32 It is possible that the US findings would not hold up in Australia. One difference is that cohabiting couples in some US states do not enjoy the same legal rights as Australian de facto couples.

33 The name in this story has been changed.

34 Kevin Andrews, 2012, *Maybe 'I Do': Modern Marriage and the Pursuit of Happiness*, Connor Court, Ballan, VIC.

35 I am grateful to Daniel Carr for reminding me of this line.

36 The survey is the 2022 HILDA survey. I opt to use wealth rather than income because income is likely to be strongly affected by family size (through the channel of parental labour supply). Having said this, saved income becomes wealth, so reverse causation is still likely to be an issue. For this sample of respondents, the poorest wealth quintile is women with household wealth below $718,200, while the top wealth quintile is women with household wealth above $3,206,115. Average numbers of children across the five wealth quintiles are 2.6, 2.2, 2.1, 2.1 and 2.3.

37 On books, see Suzanne M. Bianchi and John P. Robinson, 1997, 'What Did You Do Today? Children's Use of Time, Family Composition, and the Acquisition of Social Capital', *Journal of Marriage and the Family*, Vol. 59, No. 2, pp. 332–344. On sleep, see Mona El-Sheikh et al., 2010, 'Children's Sleep and Adjustment over Time: The Role of Socioeconomic Context', *Child Development*, Vol. 81, No. 3, pp. 870–883.

38 On corporal punishment, see Gary W. Evans, 2004, 'The Environment of Childhood Poverty', *American Psychologist*, Vol. 59, No. 2, pp. 77–92. On television, see Bianchi and Robinson, 'What Did You Do Today?' (see note 37, Chapter 6).

39 Betty Hart and Todd R. Risley, 1995, *Meaningful Differences in the Everyday Experiences of Young American Children*, Brookes, Baltimore, MD, p. 239.

40 Hank Bounds, Mississippi commissioner of higher education, quoted in Shaila Dewan, 2010, 'Southern Schools Mark Two Majorities', *The New York Times*, 6 January.

41 Department of Families, Housing, Community Services and Indigenous Affairs, 2012, *Growing Up in Australia: the Longitudinal Study of Australian Children: 2010–11 Annual Report*, FaHCSIA, Canberra, pp. 20–21.

42 Department of Families, Housing, Community Services and Indigenous Affairs, 2012, *Growing Up in Australia: The Longitudinal Study of Australian Children: 2010–11 Annual Report*, FaHCSIA, Canberra, pp. 16–17.

43 Ariel Kalil et al., 2012, 'Maternal Education and the Developmental Gradient in Time with Children: Evidence from Australia', PowerPoint Presentation, Melbourne Institute, Melbourne, 26 July.

44 Annette Lareau, 2003, *Unequal Childhoods*, University of California Press, Berkeley, CA.
45 Ibid. See also Malcolm Gladwell, 2008, *Outliers: The Story of Success*, Little, Brown & Co., New York. Because parenting styles are never randomly distributed, we can't be perfectly sure of the causal link between a particular parenting approach and children's outcomes – but the correlations certainly appear strong.
46 Susan Mayer, 1997, *What Money Can't Buy: Family Income and Children's Life Chances*, Harvard University Press, Cambridge, MA.
47 In Canada and Denmark, one study found that 30–40 per cent of young adults had at some point been employed at the same firm as their fathers: Paul Bingley, Miles Corak and Niels C. Westergård-Nielsen, 2012, 'The Intergenerational Transmission of Employers in Canada and Denmark', in John Ermisch, Markus Jantti and Timothy Smeeding (eds), *From Parents to Children: The Intergenerational Transmission of Advantage*, Russell Sage, New York.
48 See the literature review in D'Addio, 'Intergenerational Mobility' (see note 26, Chapter 6), p. 208. One of the best ways of learning about genetic effects is to look at the influence of biological and adoptive parents on the outcomes of adoptee children: see, for example, Anders Björklund, Mikael Lindahl and Erik Plug, 2006, 'The Origins of Intergenerational Associations: Lessons from Swedish Adoption Data', *Quarterly Journal of Economics*, Vol. 121, No. 3, pp. 999–1028.
49 On the height effect, see Michael Kortt and Andrew Leigh, 2010, 'Does Size Matter in Australia?', *Economic Record*, Vol. 86, pp. 71–83.
50 For a useful review of this literature (and a critique of the genetic determinism inherent in Richard Herrnstein and Charles Murray, 1994, *The Bell Curve*, Free Press, New York), see James Heckman, 2012, 'Promoting Social Mobility', *Boston Review*, Vol. 37, No. 5, pp. 14–34.
51 In Year 9, Australian children with a higher educated parent have test scores that place them nearly a year ahead of children with a lower educated parent: D'Addio, 'Intergenerational Mobility' (see note 26, Chapter 6), p. 211.
52 This account comes from 'Sarah', whose story of an unexpected pregnancy is told earlier in the chapter.
53 The most affluent fifth of Australians spend 2.6 times as much money on their children as the poorest fifth: Brenton Holmes, 2012, *Character: A Personal and Public Good*, Broad Press, Canberra, p. 119.
54 Tuomas Pekkarinen, Roope Uusitalo and Sari Pekkala, 2006, 'Education Policy and Intergenerational Income Mobility: Evidence from the Finnish Comprehensive School Reform', IZA Discussion Paper 2204, Institute for the Study of Labor (IZA), Bonn.
55 A quick web search reveals a host of elite non-government schools that provide special entry to the children of alumni, including Melbourne Grammar School, Pymble Ladies' College, Abbotsleigh, and St Ignatius' College, Riverview.
56 Juan Baron, Deborah Cobb-Clark and Nisvan Erkal, 2009, 'Cultural Transmission of Work–Welfare Attitudes and the Intergenerational

Correlation in Welfare Receipt', ANU CEPR Discussion Paper 594, ANU, Canberra, p. 28.

57 Attitudes of other types might matter too. For example, one Irish study showed that – holding grades constant – university students from disadvantaged backgrounds expected to earn less money when they graduated: Liam Delaney, Colm Harmon and Cathy Redmond, 2011, 'Parental Education, Grade Attainment and Earnings Expectations among University Students', *Economics of Education Review*, Vol. 30, pp. 1136– 1152.

58 Dalton, *Some Aspects of the Inequality of Incomes in Modern Communities* (see note 39, Chapter 5), pp. 21–22.

Chapter 7

1 David Neal et al., 2011, 'Australian Attitudes towards Wealth Inequality and Progressive Taxation', Report prepared for the Australian Council of Trade Unions, ACTU, Melbourne. The survey asked respondents what they thought the actual and ideal distribution of wealth across quintiles should be.

2 The US survey found that the average respondent thought the top quintile had 59 per cent of wealth, where the true figure is 84 per cent. See Michael Norton and Dan Ariely, 2011, 'Building a Better America – One Wealth Quintile at a Time', *Perspectives in Psychological Science*, Vol. 6, pp. 9–12.

3 Norton and Ariely, 'Building a Better America' (see note 2, Chapter 7).

4 Survey estimates were tabulated from Nicola McNeil, Ann Evans, Steve McEachern, Bruce Tranter and Shaun Wilson, 2020, *Australian Survey of Social Attitudes 2019*. All analysis uses population weights. Actual unskilled earnings are from ABS, 2019, *Employee Earnings and Hours 2018*, Cat. No. 6306.0, Data Cube 13. I take the estimate of total cash earnings of the occupation 'Packers and product assemblers' ($1015 per week). Board chair earnings are from the Australian Board Remuneration Survey, conducted by the Governance Institute, in collaboration with McGuirk Management Consultants.

5 National Social Science Survey 1994 and Australian Survey of Social Attitudes 2019. I have reported the share of people who 'strongly agree' or 'agree', with the remainder saying that they 'neither agree nor disagree', 'disagree' or 'strongly disagree'.

6 Results are from the Australian Survey of Social Attitudes 2019 and the International Social Science Program's *Social Inequality* surveys. The share saying 'strongly agree' or 'agree' (as distinct from 'neither agree nor disagree', 'disagree' or 'strongly disagree') was 29 per cent in 1987, 25 per cent in 1992 and 20 per cent in 1999.

7 Australian Survey of Social Attitudes 2019.

8 OECD, 2021, *Does Inequality Matter? How People Perceive Economic Disparities and Social Mobility*, OECD Publishing, Paris.

9 Ibid.

10 Results are from the Australian Survey of Social Attitudes 2019. Pyramid-shaped distributions are those labelled Type A ('A small elite at the top, very few people in the middle and the great mass of people at the bottom'), Type B ('A society like a pyramid with a small elite at the top, more people in the

middle and the most at the bottom') and Type C ('A pyramid except that just a few people are at the bottom'). The other two alternatives are Type D ('A society with most people in the middle') and Type E ('Many people near the top, and only a few near the bottom').

11 Australian Survey of Social Attitudes 2019. The share of people who say that the Australian income distribution matches one of the pyramid shapes was 74 per cent in 1992, 67 per cent in 1999 and 57 per cent in 2009 (International Social Science Program's *Social Inequality* surveys).

12 In 1987, 22 per cent of respondents thought one of the pyramid-shaped income distributions was ideal (International Social Science Program, 1987, *Social Inequality I*).

13 The share putting themselves in each class is lower class 4.7 per cent, working class 22.7 per cent, lower middle class 17.9 per cent, middle class 45.6 per cent, upper middle class 7.8 per cent, and upper class 1.3 per cent: Australian Survey of Social Attitudes 2019.

14 Going from bottom to top, the percentage placing themselves in each decile was 1.9, 1.4, 5.2, 8.6, 25.6, 26.9, 18.0, 10.1, 1.2 and 1.2 per cent respectively: Australian Survey of Social Attitudes 2019.

15 I am grateful to Paul Kauffman for conversations about this passage.

16 Sarah Cameron and Ian McAllister, 2022, *Trends in Australian Political Opinion: Results from the Australian Election Study 1987– 2022*, Australian National University, Canberra, p.116. Figure 14 recalculates these estimates, omitting those who did not answer the question one way or the other.

17 By contrast, the share of Britons who agree that 'the government should redistribute income' fell from around one-half in the early 1990s to around one-third in the early 2000s, then rose to around one-half in the early 2020s: Susan Butt, Elizabeth Clery and John Curtice (eds), 2022, *British Social Attitudes: The 39th Report*, National Centre for Social Research, London.

18 Cameron and McAllister, *Trends in Australian Political Opinion: Results from the Australian Election Study 1987– 2022* (see note 16, Chapter 7), pp. 115. Figure 14 recalculates these estimates, omitting those who did not answer the question one way or the other. The question about government spending was not asked in 1990.

19 The share who agreed with the statement that the government has a responsibility to reduce income gaps was 52 per cent in the 2009 Australian Survey of Social Attitudes and 47 per cent in the 2011 Australian Survey of Social Attitudes.

20 Australian Survey of Social Attitudes 2019.

21 A 2012 survey found that 62 per cent of Australians thought that 'most rich people deserve their wealth', significantly above the global average of 39 per cent: 'Rich and Infamous', *The Economist*, 11 July 2012 (based on a GlobeScan poll of 12,000 people in twenty-three countries). Survey data on whether people with high incomes should pay more tax are from the Australian Survey of Social Attitudes 2019.

22 Norberto Bobbio, 1996, *Left and Right: The Significance of a Political Distinction*, Polity Press, Cambridge, pp. 68–69.

23 For example, the Labor Party's national conference passed resolutions opposing the Imperial honours system in 1918, 1921, 1930 and 1955: see Encel, *Equality and Authority* (see note 7, Introduction), p. 129.

24 This is based on the 2022 Australian Election Study. Among those who gave their first preference vote in the House of Representatives to the Labor Party, 64 per cent agreed that income and wealth should be redistributed, 10 per cent disagreed, and 26 per cent neither agreed nor disagreed. Among Coalition voters, 36 per cent agreed, 33 per cent disagreed, and 31 per cent neither agreed nor disagreed (survey responses are weighted to match the Australian 18+ citizen population).

25 This is based on the 2019 Australian Candidates Study (the Study was not conducted in 2022). For Labor candidates, 82.5 per cent agreed, 2.5 per cent disagreed, and 15 per cent neither agreed nor disagreed. For Coalition candidates, 7 per cent agreed, 83 per cent disagreed, and 10 per cent neither agreed nor disagreed. Matching this, one estimate found that Coalition members tend to be richer than Labor members. A 2010 study using data from the register of members' interests put average wealth per MP at $4.9 million for Liberal MPs, $1.7 million for Labor MPs, $1.4 million for National Party MPs and $1.1 million for Independent MPs. Excluding the two MPs with the highest household wealth (Malcolm Turnbull and Kevin Rudd), the Liberal average fell to $1.6 million, while the Labor average fell to $1 million. See Gillian Tan, 2010, 'Members Reap Rewards of High Office', *BRW* magazine, 27 May. Note that the estimates are likely to be quite imprecise, given that the register of members' interests does not provide dollar values for properties, mortgages, shareholdings and the like.

26 Anthony Albanese, 2017, 'Positive Politics in the Age of Disruption', 34th Annual Earle Page Political Lecture, University of New England, Armidale, 18 July; Jim Chalmers, 2013, First Speech, House of Representatives, 13 November.

27 Wayne Swan, 2012, 'Land of Hope and Dreams', John Button Lecture, Melbourne, 1 August. See also Wayne Swan, 2012, 'The 0.01 per cent: The Rising Influence of Vested Interests in Australia', *The Monthly*, March. Other prominent Labor parliamentarians to have focused on inequality include Craig Emerson, 1999, 'Inequality: Problems and Solutions', *The Sydney Papers*, Vol. 11, No. 4, pp. 89–106 and Lindsay Tanner, 2012, *Politics with Purpose: Occasional Observations on Public and Private Life*, Scribe, Melbourne.

28 John Howard, 2004, 'Joint Press Conference with Brendan Nelson', Canberra, 11 March 2004, cited in Tom Conley, 2004, 'Globalisation and Rising Inequality in Australia: Is Increasing Inequality Inevitable in Australia?', Paper presented to the Australasian Political Science Association annual meetings.

29 Cited in Mike Steketee, 2003, 'Still Work in Progress', *The Australian*, 7 June, p. 22.

30 Robert Menzies, 1942, 'The Forgotten People', Radio broadcast, 22 May; Joe Hockey, 2014, Budget Speech, 13 May.

31 My own speeches account for 124 of the 2918 mentions of inequality in federal parliamentary debates from 2010 to 2024 (4 per cent of the total).

32 So far as I am aware, no one has published estimates of the total number of sittings hours per year for the Senate and House of Representatives combined (at least not on an annual basis since 1901). I therefore use a different approach, which is to find a word that is used frequently in *Hansard*, and whose regularity has not changed since 1901. I opt for the word 'Wednesday' (results are similar if I use 'Tuesday', 'Speaker' or 'Hansard'). Dividing the number of times 'inequality' is mentioned by the number of times 'Wednesday' is mentioned provides an estimate of the frequency of debates over inequality. This figure is then multiplied by 100 for ease of interpretation. Figure 15 shows a five-year moving average, except in the first two years and the last two years, where the average only covers the current year plus the two subsequent (or prior) years.

33 See, for example, Hugh Mackay's *Mind and Mood* reports over this period.

34 For a useful history, see Andrew Herscovitch and David Stanton, 2008, 'History of Social Security in Australia', *Family Matters*, No. 80, pp. 51–60.

35 The pension assets test had been abolished by Malcolm Fraser's Coalition government in 1976. Legislation to reintroduce the pension assets test was foreshadowed in the 1983 budget, and introduced into parliament in 1984. Peacock quotes are from the *House of Representatives Hansard*, 17 November 1983 ('callous and cynical') and 7 June 1984 ('assaults on the elderly').

36 'Penalising thrift' quote from Senator Messner, the shadow social security spokesperson, is from the *Senate Hansard*, 17 August 1984.

37 Australian Treasury, 2020, *The JobKeeper Payment: Three-Month Review*, Australian Treasury, Canberra, p.50; Ownership Matters, 2020, 'JobKeeper and other government subsidies', Ownership Matters, Melbourne, 9 September.

38 Baby Bonus statistics from Wayne Swan, 2008, 'Means Testing Report Misleading,' Media Release, 18 May. Turnbull quote is from the *House of Representatives Hansard*, 14 May 2008.

39 Joe Hockey interview with Greg Cary, 4BC Brisbane, 11 May 2011.

40 The frontbencher was Christopher Pyne, quoted in Lenore Taylor, 2012, 'Perspective the First Casualty of Budget Backlash', *The Age*, 23 October. Hockey's statement is from a *Lateline* interview with Emma Alberici on 22 October 2012, in which he said 'the Government seems to want to penalise anyone that has a second or third child. I think that worked quite well in China, didn't it?'.

41 Albert Métin, 2012 [1901], 'The Workers Paradise', in *The Words that Made Australia* (see note 31, Chapter 1).

42 This point is made in John Hirst, 2003, *Australia's Democracy: A Short History*, Allen and Unwin, Sydney, p. 311. Hirst notes that Boer War memorials are the exception, as they list officers first.

43 Field Marshal Viscount Allenby, quoted in Encel, *Equality and Authority* (see note 7, Introduction), p. 433.

44 On 14 February 1914, Australian soldiers from Casula Camp went on strike to protest excessive training hours, marching through the streets of Liverpool and the Sydney CBD: Carl Reinecke, 2010, 'The Other Charge of the Light Brigade', *Griffith Review*, Edition 28, pp. 226–231. Other strikes

occurred after the order on 23 September 1918 to disband six Australian battalions to reinforce others: see Charles Bean, 1942, *Official History of Australia in the War of 1914–1918*, Volume VI, first edition, pp. 937–940 (though Bean prefers to call the soldiers' strikes 'mutinies'). The other country to have experienced army mutinies is France, which also has a strong egalitarian tradition.

45 Writing in 1964, Donald Horne described the situation as: 'Whatever kind of a bastard the boss might be, he usually rolls up his sleeves and looks like one of the boys ... Ordinary Australians no longer envy their bosses ... They attribute success to good luck ... Ordinary people are not concerned with the ways of the rich.' Horne, *The Lucky Country* (see note 3, Chapter 6), p. 12.

46 Focus group participant quoted in Hugh Mackay, 1992, *What Do I Believe In?* Mackay Research, Sydney, p. 47.

Chapter 8

1 Hirst, *The Australians* (see note 1, Introduction), p. 1.

2 Christopher Joye, 2012, 'Egalitarian Distribution of Income Is Destructive', *Australian Financial Review*, 25 September.

3 Weights in the Kentucky Derby are allocated based on the sex of the horse, with entry restricted to three-year-olds.

4 Quoted in Encel, *Equality and Authority* (see note 7, Introduction), p. 49. This was partly due to the Victorian government's decision to prescribe a small claim size on the diggings, which increased the number of people who had access to the 'lottery': see Ian McLean, 2013, *Why Australia Prospered: The Shifting Sources of Economic Growth*, Princeton University Press, Princeton, NJ.

5 Francis Adams, 1886, *Australian Essays*, W. Inglis, London, p. 33.

6 Joseph Furphy, 1903, *Such Is Life: Being Certain Extracts from the Diary of Tom Collins*, Bulletin Newspaper Company, Sydney, p. 117, quoted in Encel, *Equality and Authority* (see note 7, Introduction), p. 50.

7 Hugh Mackay, 1998, *Class and Status*, Mackay Research, Sydney, p. 13.

8 This analogy is used by Harvard philosopher Michael Sandel in his lectures on 'Justice'.

9 These estimates are based on Australian Curriculum, Assessment and Reporting Authority 2023, *NAPLAN National Results 2023 (Excel File)*, ACARA, Sydney.

10 Estimates from the Longitudinal Survey of Youth suggest that a young person in the lowest socioeconomic quartile is 20 percentage points less likely to finish Year 12 than someone from the highest socioeconomic quartile: Robinson and Lamb, *How Young People Are Faring 2012* (see note 35, Chapter 4), p. 52.

11 A similar widening of achievement gaps between advantaged and disadvantaged students has taken place in the US: Jason DeParle, 2012, 'For Many Poor Students, Leap to College Ends in a Hard Fall', *The New York Times*, 23 December, p. A1.

12 For a thoughtful discussion of the effect of industrial relations law changes on the operations of unions, see Jeff Borland, 2012, 'Industrial Relations

Reform: Chasing a Pot of Gold at the End of the Rainbow?', Lecture given at the University of Melbourne, 19 March.

13 The drop in Brazilian inequality coincided with the presidency from 2003–2010 of Luiz Inácio Lula da Silva (aka 'Lula'), who instituted conditional cash transfers (*Bolsa Família*) and access to basic foodstuffs (*Fome Zero*). See Degol Hailu and Sergei Suarez Dillon Soares, 2009, 'What Explains the Decline in Brazil's Inequality?', *One Pager* No. 89, International Policy Centre for Inclusive Growth, Brasilia; OECD, 2015, *Brazil Policy Brief: Inequality*, OECD, Paris, November.

14 Peter Whiteford, 2010, 'The Australian Tax-Transfer System: Architecture and Outcomes', *Economic Record*, Vol. 86, No. 275, pp. 528–544. The Australian welfare system is the most progressive in the OECD because each dollar spent through it does more to reduce inequality than in any other OECD nation. But because the size of the welfare system (as a share of GDP) is smaller than in many other OECD countries, it is not the most redistributive. For example, while each dollar of Scandinavian welfare does less to reduce inequality than each dollar of Australian welfare, the Scandinavian welfare systems are so much larger than ours that they end up having a bigger overall impact on reducing inequality. For a thoughtful discussion of these issues, see also Greg Jericho, 2012 'Why the GST May Not Be Good for Us', *The Drum*, 26 September (abc.net.au/unleashed/4279782.html).

15 In recent years, these issues have been sidetracked by a debate over whether people above a particular cut-off are 'rich'. I'm personally agnostic as to whether $300,000 a year makes you rich or not. But it does put you in the top 1 per cent of individual income earners.

16 On 20 September 2009, the full single age-pension was increased from 25 to 27.7 per cent of male total average weekly earnings, an increase of more than 10 per cent, or $1689. Peter Whiteford attributes this to the drop in poverty (measured as 50 per cent of median household income) from 14 per cent in 2007–08 to 11 per cent in 2009–10: Whiteford, 'Inequality and Redistribution in the Australian Welfare State' (see note 19, Chapter 3).

17 Robert J. Shiller, 2012, *Finance and the Good Society*, Princeton University Press, Princeton, NJ.

18 Chung Tran and Nabeeh Zakariyya, 2021, 'Tax progressivity in Australia: Facts, measurements and estimates', *Economic Record*, vol. 97, no. 316, pp. 45–77., Figure 13b. Similar results are contained in Roger Wilkins, 2012, 'Do We Really Know What Happened to Income Inequality in Australia over the Last Decade?', Parliamentary Library Vital Issues Seminar, 10 October (showing a fall in the Reynolds-Smolensky index during the noughties). See also Andrew Leigh, 2005, 'Deriving Long-Run Inequality Series from Tax Data', *Economic Record*, Vol. 81, S58–S70.

19 See for example Ken Henry, 2010, *Australia's Future Tax System: Report to the Treasurer*, Australian Treasury, Canberra, Part One, p. 29.

20 Andrew Leigh, 2018, *Randomistas: How Radical Researchers Changed Our World*, Black Inc, Melbourne.

21 Australian Survey of Social Attitudes 2019.

22 For a longer case for this, see Macgregor Duncan et al., 2004, *Imagining Australia: Ideas for Our Future*, Allen and Unwin, Sydney. My hope for reclaiming Eureka was buoyed when I moved a motion in the House of Representatives about its importance, supported in spirit by members of both parties: see *House of Representatives Hansard*, 26 November 2012. I can also recommend Peter FitzSimons, 2012, *Eureka: The Unfinished Revolution*, Random House, Sydney.

23 This letter was written by Jacinta Mudge, an English student in the class of Liam Wood, a Teach for Australia associate. Thanks to Teach for Australia's Jessica Rose and Liam Wood for allowing me to quote it in this context.

Acknowledgements

1 Christopher Jencks, 1972, *Inequality: A Reassessment of the Effect of Family and Schooling in America*, Basic Books, New York; Anthony B. Atkinson, 1972, *Unequal Shares: Wealth in Britain*, Allen Lane, London.

Index